BLOWN TOGETHER

THE TRIALS AND MIRACLES OF KATRINA

Fr. Sebastian Myladiyil, SVD

Evergreen
PRESS

Mobile, Alabama

Evergreen Press
P.O. Box 191540 • Mobile, AL 36619
800-367-8203

Dedicated to the people of goodwill
who reached out to us
in the trying times after Katrina.

Table of Contents

Foreword

August 29, 2005 is a date etched in the minds and hearts of the people of the Gulf Coast. Hurricane Katrina possessed incredible force: the tidal surge caused the sea to rise 28 feet, the equivalent of a tsunami, and the winds howled with the intensity of an F-2 tornado. In a matter of a few hours the fury of Hurricane Katrina inflicted catastrophic devastation damaging and even obliterating entire neighborhoods in towns along the Gulf Coast.

The story of Katrina is more than the collective story of communities. It is also the story of the individual suffering, strength, resiliency, and faith of the people who make up the communities. Everyone who endured Katrina has his or her own story. This book, *Blown Together—Trials and Miracles of Katrina*, contains some of these moving tales. Katrina changed the landscape. But it did more. Katrina changed us. Great moments of struggle in our lives affect us. We cannot choose the time we suffer or the manner in which we suffer. We can only choose what we do with the suffering that comes into our lives and how we allow it to change us.

There is a saying, "It is only at night that we see the stars." This adage reflects the truth that it is in life's darkest times that we can see the goodness of God and neighbor that have been there all along but that in the bright times we may fail to see. For those who recognize the goodness that surrounds us, even in the most desperate of times, it is possible for suffering to change us into wiser, more compassionate, and more faith-filled people. The choice is ours. Our sufferings can make us better or can make us bitter. Our sufferings will not leave us unchanged.

I thank Father Sebastian Myladiyil for compiling these stories. From the first moments after Katrina, he not only made

Saint Rose de Lima parish a bright light in the darkness, he himself was a bright light, a star of encouragement, help, and faith to the people of Bay St. Louis and beyond. I pray that these poignant stories of the worst natural disaster to befall the United States will inspire all who encounter trials in their lives to know that miracles happen too.

—*Most Rev. Thomas J. Rodi, DD*
Archbishop, Archdiocese of Mobile, Alabama

Acknowledgments

To God be the glory! To God be the glory! To God be the glory! In the same breath, Lord, please forgive me, forgive me and forgive me. How often have I ignored your voice, your deeds and your presence. You caught my attention in a big way that I was never prepared for! I have seen Your miracles, I have felt Your love, and I have tasted Your goodness, and I am not the same.

Those who have shared the stories in this book proclaim it loud and clear that they have seen the miracles, felt Your passionate love, and tasted Your amazing goodness too. My heart is filled with gratitude for each of the contributors. They were given a very brief deadline to come up with their stories, and they responded to my plea enthusiastically. The individuals who tell their short stories are just a tiny segment in comparison to the many who were part of the large story. But their stories can heighten once again our awareness that we were not blown apart, but blown together. My sincere gratitude to each one of them.

I extend my sincere appreciation to Archbishop Thomas J. Rodi of the Archdiocese of Mobile, Alabama, for enthusiastically supporting my endeavor and delightedly agreeing to write the foreword for this book. My heart is full of gratitude for his leadership in the diocese of Biloxi particularly in the trying times after Katrina.

I am so grateful to the community of St. Rose de Lima. I came to you as a young priest, just under two years in ministry. You have helped me grow in my life and ministry. My hope and prayer is to see you continue to grow and thrive as a spirit-filled, vibrant community.

My heart is full when I think of all the good people who reached out to us. How many individuals, how many churches, how many schools, how many colleges, how many volunteers, how many organizations, how many leaders! In small or large ways, in seen or unseen manner, they have contributed to making our lives better. I am sure there are many whose names were not mentioned, there are many whose works were not acknowledged, and there are many whose efforts were not recognized. But know that your goodness, goodwill, and efforts have made a difference in our lives and ultimately have been seen by God.

I was so excited about having a publisher for this endeavor. After having a book published independently, and having experienced the pain of marketing it, I was thrilled to be connected with Evergreen Press in Mobile, Alabama. It has been a wonderful journey after making the connection.

Words cannot express my gratitude to Bruce Northridge, Tamera Whavers, Mary Coyne, and Dr. Jerald Jackson for the roles they played in editing each of my chapters and suggesting ideas to make the work holistic. Tamera Whavers has been very diligent in typing some of my notes and handwritten individual stories provided by the contributors.

My gratitude to Fr. Jaison Mangalath, SVD and Fr. Arokiam Arokiam, SVD for their amazing support in this endeavor. Your brotherly love and enthusiastic support will be remembered forever. I am forever grateful to Audrey and Dick Stermer, Westcliffe, CO, Patton & Elleen Mashburn, Diamondhead, MS, and Dr. Charles & Dot Heidingsfelder, New Orleans, LA for their support towards this undertaking.

The community of Bay-Waveland and Hancock County in Mississippi is a blessed place with a great number of wonderful individuals, great leaders, and a profound sense of unity. I thank God for the opportunity He gave me to live in this wonderful place for the last nine years.

Introduction

With the encouragement of several people and after careful reflection, I was compelled to pen my pastoral experiences over the past five years of my post-Katrina life—experiences of recovery, rebuilding, and resiliency at St. Rose de Lima Catholic Church and in the communities of Bay St. Louis, Waveland, and Hancock County. *Blown Together—Trials and Miracles of Katrina* is my humble attempt to make sure that we do not forget our experiences or ignore the lessons we learned following Katrina.

Members of St. Rose parish, the St. Rose Outreach and Recovery (SOAR) program, the volunteers who "pitched their tents" among us following the storm, as well as civic and governmental leaders have contributed to *Blown Together*, recounting their unique experiences of trials, challenges, joys, sources of strength, and miracles. These colleagues were chosen because I have personally witnessed their resilient spirits and their hope in the midst of devastation. I hope that these amazing stories will serve as a catalyst of faith, hope, and optimism in the lives of all readers.

CHAPTER 1

Our World Was Suddenly Changed

In just a few hours on August 29, 2005, life changed forever for Gulf Coast residents. The fury of Katrina left hundreds of thousands of people homeless, hundreds dead, and countless financially broken. The whole nation, and in fact the whole world, watched in horror as Katrina unleashed her fury on the Gulf Coast. People who had abundance the day before were destitute the day after. Katrina showed no partiality as she treated everyone with the same brutal force. She respected no one, and no one was immune because of economic status, gender, race, ethnic origin, educational background, social standing, or religious affiliation. All who were in her way were treated with the same harshness and cruelty.

Everyone found themselves to be in similar situations. Katrina removed the barriers that had once separated people. In this particular crisis, no differences existed between rich and poor, black and white, educated and uneducated, or men and women. Tragedies and crises have a tremendous capacity to break down barriers and bring people together. This was probably the first miracle people experienced, although it may have gone unnoticed given their overwhelming circumstances. What seemed most important in the midst of all the grief was the powerful realization that life is precious. "You are alive. I am alive. Together, we can move forward" seemed to be the unspoken motto for many.

The trials and heartaches brought about by Katrina were many. Losses included lives, friends, homes, jobs, familiar surroundings, neighbors, and communities. None of us asked for this situation. We found ourselves to be in complete chaos and disarray. All of us were trying to make sense of the mess in which we found ourselves. Yet, in the midst of such trials, many tremendous blessings have emerged . . . as have miracles large and small. So many good things have come out of the whole experience!

A miracle becomes a reality only when it is recognized. People of faith are able to see miracles happening in their lives and are capable of acknowledging the divine guidance in their endeavors. They are less inclined to say, "I was lucky" or "It was by chance." Rather, they recognize the grace of God, saying, "I am blessed" and trust that miracles do happen in their lives.

The age-old humorous story of the elderly woman comes to my mind. She was poor and helpless and in many ways depended upon the generosity of other people for her survival. Upon receiving help, she would thank those who gave and would praise God saying, "All glory to God who made this happen!" Her atheist neighbor was very annoyed at her claim and used to tease her that she was naïve and ignorant. He claimed that she was giving undue praise. His protestations did not bother her, and she continued to claim it was God who made things happen in her life.

One day the atheist neighbor decided to bring her some supplies and leave them on the front porch of her home. She was certainly overjoyed and gave praise to God for this "miracle" in her life. The man came forward with a condescending laugh, saying, "Ha! God had nothing to do with it. I was the one who brought those things to you." She looked at him and said, "I know it was God, because I know He can use anyone to help me. This time, He has chosen the devil to come my aid!"

Humor aside, when we focus on the message of the story, one thing becomes clear—God can use anyone to bring about His purpose, even without that person's knowledge. Many people who came to our aid after Katrina might not claim that God moved them to act, but the results of their actions were clear signs of God's goodness, kindness, generosity, graciousness, and love at work. As recipients of people's graciousness, I can say those actions were miracles to behold because they were God's work through people.

I have heard several people echoing the same sentiment, "If not for our faith, where would we be?" They were actually asserting the reality of miracles happening in their lives in the midst of the pain and suffering. Those were moments when no rational explanation helped the person deal with those challenges. Only when people were able to connect their faith with the challenges at hand did they realize the strength of conviction needed to face their trials. Faith has this tremendous capacity to awaken greater energy in a person's being as he or she is assured of a supernatural power at work in the given situation. For me, the resiliency of the human spirit is a loud and clear exhibition of miracle in someone's life.

Katrina caused tremendous destruction, pain, and suffering. Yes, our world as we knew it had suddenly changed. Many were able to recognize miracles that happened in their lives—either right at the moment or days, months, or even years after the ordeal. We learned that we could not do it on our own. We needed one another and we needed God.

CHAPTER 2

Disturb Me, O Lord,
When I Am Too Comfortable

I was having the best time of my life. I came to St. Rose in June 2001 and soon made this vibrant community my new home. As a newly ordained priest in the Society of the Divine Word, I had come to this wonderful country from India in August 1999. My pastoral experience was limited to a short stay at St. Edwards / St. Jude Church in New Iberia, Louisiana, for less than two years. I had a wonderful mentor in Fr. Thomas James, SVD, who introduced me to various aspects of parish life. The community embraced me immediately, and I found my ministry thriving there in Louisiana. I then received a transfer in June 2001 to be pastor at St. Rose de Lima in Bay St. Louis, Mississippi.

I joyfully anticipated my new assignment at St. Rose. The historically African-American church was founded in 1926 and was well known for its open-mindedness, powerful liturgies, wonderful gospel choir, and breathtaking sanctuary adorned with a mural of Christ in the Oaks. Its committed, strong leaders and members were passionate about their church and

4

fearless in addressing issues, which also made me nervous to take on this assignment!

While I possessed knowledge and experience in the pastoral and sacramental aspects of a parish, I had limited knowledge of its administrative dimension. Further, I was succeeding a seasoned, well-known and beloved priest—Fr. Francis Theriault, SVD—and I was only twenty-nine years old. Upon my arrival, leaders at St. Rose welcomed me and challenged me saying that I had big shoes to fill. I would jokingly respond, "I wear an eight-and-a-half." I knew the people at St. Rose had great expectations of me.

God has His way of making things happen in our lives. Soon I found myself accepted in the parish and in the larger community. We set in motion plans for improving various areas of the church such as liturgy, ministry, organizational structure, volunteerism, and capital projects (primarily the building of a community center, which had been a dream of the parish for many years). As a pastor, I knew the importance and value of getting to know members of the parish from a personal perspective; that is, to know their stories, dreams, hardships, and their hopes for St. Rose. From that emerged my plan to get to know everyone by visiting every person in the parish and blessing each home.

The idea was well-received. During my first year as pastor, I sat at the table with more than one hundred individuals/families, listening to their stories and sharing dreams of the future of St. Rose. It became clear within months that we could take the parish to a new level if we raised the standard for all. Of course, as usual, some resisted change and wanted to keep things as they were. However, a vast majority wanted to move ahead with new plans for the community.

St. Rose is an integral part of the larger community, and I

soon became a part of several boards and organizations, which brought added exposure to the parish. I truly loved the people and the place. I was simply thrilled to be able to contribute to the betterment of the community in so many small ways.

By the first part of 2005, many personal and shared dreams were coming true. Our parish had a great vitality expressed in our liturgies and our Bible study groups. Various groups and individuals were becoming highly engaged in their ministries, and our members were empowered by the spirit of hope at St. Rose and in our surrounding neighborhoods.

We launched our Capital Campaign and were flooded with generous donations and pledges from parishioners as well as other people. March 19, 2005 was the groundbreaking date for the new parish center. We were confident we had made it and were moving forward.

On a personal level, I had the desire to continue my studies to obtain a Master's degree. It looked very feasible for me to enroll in a university and at the same time manage the pastoral and administrative tasks of the parish. I told myself if we could complete the construction of the parish center by 2006 and finish my degree program, I could go home to India and officiate the wedding of my baby brother, Robin, and celebrate my parents' forty-fifth wedding anniversary.

Yes, my life was going wonderfully great, and I could not ask for anything better. I was comfortable and content in my life and ministry. I truly understand when people say they wish they had the power to reverse time. Though I know better, I might be tempted to want to take life back to where it was before August 29, 2005.

I came across a prayer that said, "Comfort me, O Lord, when I am in distress; but disturb me, O Lord, when I am too comfortable." I didn't offer this particular prayer in my life at any time fervently, but events that happened with Hurricane Katrina in many ways made this prayer sensible.

CHAPTER 3

It Didn't Come at a Good Time

The storm brewing in the Atlantic Ocean and meandering across the Caribbean seemed likely to lose its strength and wither away into a tropical storm or go elsewhere. But as the probability of the storm hitting the Gulf Coast became more evident in the days that followed, an air of anxiety soon began to grip the community. Still, many people seemed to go about their routine business as hurricane alerts are a normal part of coastal living.

The diocesan directives for evacuation were perfectly clear. Priests were given the option to cancel weekend Masses and evacuate to safe places. Because the storm was predicted to hit the Coast on Sunday night or Monday morning, it made perfect sense to announce the cancellation of services and move to a safe location. But, being my stubborn self, I decided to wait and see how things might play out. I decided to have all the weekend Masses. Weekends are a busy time in a priest's life and certainly not the right time for a storm to arrive!

I celebrated all three weekend Masses. Saturday evening Mass was well-attended. However, several people informed me as they were leaving the church that they were evacuating and pleaded with me to do the same. Projecting great confidence, I told them that I preferred to stay rather than go through the congested traffic and the all the hassles of moving. In the previous four years I had evacuated a few times, only to find everything intact upon my return. I made my decision this time to stay in Bay St. Louis.

On Sunday morning as I got out of bed and said my short morning prayers, I asked for protection upon everyone on the Gulf Coast. Then I turned on the television only to hear about a "perfect storm" fast approaching us. Even though people who normally were at the 9:00 a.m. Mass were present at the 7:00 a.m. Mass, attendance was poor, and I knew many had already evacuated. When Paul and Florence Jordan, two of St. Rose' parishioners, told me after the Mass that they were leaving town, I teasingly said, "Don't be chickens, you can take it." To my horror, I later found out that they took my words seriously and decided to stay; they had to break open the roof of their house to escape the rising water!

When I went back to the rectory after the 7:00 a.m. Mass, I knew things were much more serious than I had anticipated, but I held onto the hope that the storm would lose its power or go away. When I called my home in India, my brother, Robin, inquired about the seriousness of the bad weather. I assured him that it was just another storm, and there was nothing to worry about. I returned to the church for the 9.00 a.m. Mass, which was attended by only about forty to fifty members in comparison with our usual standing room only attendance. Only a few members of the Gospel Choir were present; but as usual, they sang the songs with great gusto and led the congregation in worship.

As part of the opening prayer, I selected the following

prayer from the Sacramentary (the prayer book for the Mass), entitled, "To Avert Storms." The prayer goes like this:

> Father, all the elements of nature obey Your command.
> Calm the storms that threaten us and
> Turn our fear of Your power into praise of Your goodness.
> Grant this through our Lord Jesus Christ, Your Son,
> Who lives and reigns with You and the Holy Spirit,
> One God, forever and ever. Amen.

I also concluded the liturgy with the same prayer. Little did I know my decision to use this prayer would become a powerful motivating factor for the rest of my life and ministry! This I will remember forever.

As I always did at the end of the Mass, I greeted everyone, assured mutual prayers for one another, and proceeded to do a final check on all the buildings. When I went back to the rectory and looked at the Weather Channel, my anxiety began to grow. I called my classmate and friend, Fr. Jaison Magalath, SVD, who advised me to leave Bay St. Louis. Reluctantly I agreed and went to make the final preparations. As per the diocesan guidelines, I took the Holy Eucharist and all the important parish registers with me along with a few personal items and left the city for Baton Rouge, Louisiana.

Once I reached I-10, I could see the slow-moving traffic. The drive became worse when I reached I-12, which was closed to the west; all the traffic was being redirected towards Hattiesburg. As I had no one to go to in Hattiesburg, I decided to turn around and come back to the Bay. I took the Eucharist back to the tabernacle in the church and placed all the registers back into the safe in the parish office. When I called Fr. James Pawlicki, SVD at St. Augustine Seminary, he asked me to come over to the seminary to ride out the storm. St. Augustine Seminary had never been flooded as it is located on some of the highest ground in Bay St. Louis. A few priests and brothers in active ministry, as well as several retired priests, lived there. Soon I left the ready-for-demolition old wooden framed rectory at St. Rose to stay at a stronger and newer building at the seminary.

Chapter 4

The Storm Hits

The evening was very pleasant. St. Augustine seminary was always a happy place for me. Even though anxiety lingered in the air, we pretended to have things under control. The benchmark until then was Hurricane Camille of 1969 that did not cause serious damage to St. Augustine seminary. We felt that we were all in a safe place. We were a bunch of holy priests who had given our lives to God, so it seemed right to bargain with God to protect us. For quite a while we all sat outside and talked. When I look back, those evening hours were truly "the calm before the storm."

I had already placed my small suitcase that contained a few personal belongings in a room upstairs. As night approached, all of us retreated to our respective rooms. I tried to say my evening prayers, but I was distracted in many ways. As I lay down to sleep, I begged God for protection upon the whole land.

Not too many hours had passed before I awoke to the sound of howling winds. Minutes later, the electricity was gone. In the dark, I made my way to the dining room to find a few other members already congregated there.

This is it, I thought. I was going to witness what I had heard about from the time I arrived in this area in 1999—a hurricane. I was hoping it might be limited to some powerful wind, maybe a few broken trees, and some heavy rain. None of us paid attention to the passing of time. It was a welcome relief to realize that dawn was not too far away. What lie ahead in the next few hours was never imagined, even in my wildest dreams! This was the first time in my life that I experienced the fury and wrath of nature. The wind was like nothing I had ever seen before. The sound was frightening, as was the power of the rain. Objects were flying through the air just as one would see in a movie. Everyone present had anxious looks on their faces. Prayers were uttered at frequent intervals, and all hoped that the agony would soon be over.

When I look back, I cannot say that I was afraid. There were things to be done for the retired priests. A few windows had already given out, and we began to see leaks at several locations in the buildings. Several of us who were able began moving around inside the buildings trying to fix things or protect any items inside the buildings as best we could. And we were, of course, watching the raging storm the whole time.

What was most alarming was the sudden increase of water on the ground, which was more than what the most torrential rain could have brought. Soon, the realization set in that the whole area was going to be flooded. I had never seen anything like it in my life. Dozens of cars that were parked all around the buildings and the soccer field were being tossed about as toys. Soon we began to see water seeping in through the doors into the building.

The first challenge was to get all the retired priests up to the second floor. All who were able to move by themselves did so gracefully. The rest were given assistance up the stairs. Water was all around the buildings. Looking through the window on the second floor, all I could see was the rising water; the gulf had surrounded us. This was something that no one had expected. Yes, we were ready for the wind, but nobody thought the water and tidal surge would be so powerful.

I ran from the residence area to the administrative section so I could check out how my Ford Taurus was doing. I had just completed the sixty-thousand-mile servicing and repairs, which cost me thirteen hundred dollars just the week before, and it was being tossed about by the storm. I noticed the driver's side window had rolled down (it was a built-in safety mechanism, I was told—in case the car is submerged, the driver can come out through it), and water had reached its top. Suddenly I was grateful that I had chosen to take the parish records and registers out of the car and place them in the safe at St. Rose. Standing at what I thought was the highest point in Bay St. Louis, and seeing that it seemed to be several feet under water, I did not even want to imagine what might be going on at St. Rose. I thought about all the people I had come to care about since my coming to this place, and I prayed for them. Everyone shared this struggle, I realized, and I began praying for all of those affected, even for those I had never met.

I went back to the main building and joined others who were looking out anxiously to see when the water might subside. But for several minutes, which seemed like hours, the water level kept rising outside. We all stood in a daze—watching, praying, and speaking positive words in order to calm everyone in the room. By then the director of the William J. Kelley Retreat Center, Fr. Robert Fisher, SVD had managed to swim across and reach the main building of the seminary where we were all anxiously riding out the storm. To our great alarm, he informed us that the Retreat Center had over six feet of water in all the buildings, and dozens of people from the area had taken shelter there. We were also really worried about our Provincial Fr. Joseph Simon, whose house was adjacent to the retreat center.

A full hour must have passed before we began to see the water level on the outside recede. In the meantime, two feet of water filled the main building. The quick receding of the water brought a moment of great joy to us. Our immediate desire was to get the water that was in the building to flow outside. We pried open the doors that until then we had tried to keep closed, and all who were able to do any kind of work were looking for mops and buckets to clean the first floor. The water had left behind a tremendous amount of black silt and mud that seemed to get stickier with every passing minute.

By then Fr. Simon, who was committed to ride out the storm by himself, managed to come over to the seminary, wet and shivering. We were also told that all who took shelter in the retreat center were safe, and thank God, no casualties were sustained on the seminary grounds.

I vividly recall meeting a young Chinese exchange student who had arrived in the U.S. barely a week before and was staying with an elderly couple in their home in Bay St. Louis. During the storm and as waters rose, the threesome had retreated to the roof of their home and hung onto trees until the wind died down and the waters subsided. They half-swam, half-waded to the seminary. I can still remember the excitement in their voices when they first reached the seminary and found people alive there.

Once in seeming safety, the young girl began to cry and yell at the same time as she recounted (in Chinese) the traumatizing events that she had endured. Her pain was our pain. Here she was a stranger in a foreign land who had lost all of her possessions, gone through a near-death experience, endured physical and mental agony for hours against nature's fury, and now realized she had nothing left. It was painful to experience this with her; and at the time, I did not know I would face several similar situations in the future.

Now, what? we all seemed to wonder. As far as our eyes could see, the whole area looked like a war zone. (Several days later, some of the National Guardsmen informed me they'd seen war zones that looked better!) As soon as I could place my feet on solid ground, I tried to walk to St. Rose; but fallen trees, power lines, and debris made my trip too difficult. With a heavy heart, I returned to the seminary.

That night (a Monday) was agonizing. My bed on the second floor was soaked with water leaking from the roof. No form of communication was available. No one knew the level of destruction elsewhere.

We were surrounded by devastation although we did not know its extent. We could very well imagine the possibility of loss of life. It was frightening to think about the aged and sick who might have decided to stay and ride out the storm. I hoped that most had not been hardheaded like me and decided to stay. Sleep was impossible due to the many thoughts racing through my mind, particularly the people I had come to know and love since my arrival at St. Rose in 2001. I tried to say a prayer for all of them, hoping against hope that no lives were lost.

CHAPTER 5

The Calm After the Storm

On Tuesday morning, I set out to conduct my initial damage assessment of St. Rose. After climbing over mountains of fallen trees, power lines, and shattered parts of houses, I spotted our steeple. Joy, thanksgiving, and relief filled my soul. As I approached, I could see the roof was severely damaged, and windows were either broken or blown into the building. To my amazement, the front glass doors facing the Gulf were still intact. I was able to use my keys to open the church. My eyes rested on the mural that depicted the towering image of Jesus with His outstretched arms as if to embrace me right there. I started my way up to the sanctuary.

The entire carpet at the back of the church was drenched from the water that had poured in through the damaged roof and the broken windows; ceiling tiles, prayer books, torn Bibles, and hymnals were scattered everywhere. However, as I walked halfway up the aisle, I could see little damage to the front portion and sanctuary area of the church. I walked over to the altar and found the sacramentary (prayer book for the Mass) that I had left open. The book that I had left open remained in the exact same place and the prayer "To Avert Storms" was facing me.

Words cannot describe my feelings right then as I knelt down before my awesome God with my heart welling with grateful emotions. That was a powerful moment that I can look back at for the rest of my life. I truly felt that I was in the almighty embrace of God's love and sensed confirmation of the strength of God. Suddenly I was not anxious any longer. I cannot describe the energy I was feeling in my body and in my whole being. I felt empowered by the whole experience, and I knew right then and there things would be okay. In fact, things were okay.

More miracles were in store as I left the church and went across to the school buildings. All the shades of the front school building were down, and a number of windows were broken with tangled up blinds. I was able to use my keys and open the main door of the school building. I walked into my office. It was a sharp contrast to what was outside. My normally messy office looked immaculate with no signs of damage, except for some water that had come in from the roof or seeped through the wall.

There was substantial damage in the main parish office, as the bricks from the adjacent building had collapsed onto the window air conditioning unit and had caved the wall into the office. Debris was all around, yet it appeared to be salvageable. I walked around the school building assessing damages, and I found that the back wall of one of our school buildings had also collapsed, causing severe damage to both school buildings and the breezeway. All the skylights were blown out, and the churning wind had wreaked havoc on the dropped ceiling and the insulation above the ceiling tiles, making it wet and sagging at different locations.

My next stop was the rectory, the priest's residence. I could see the wooden structure that had served as my carport had collapsed, the roof of the carport was detached and blown over onto the roof of the house, and the laundry room was in complete disarray. Walking carefully through the nails, shingles, metal pieces, and wood, I was able to open the door and find the rectory more or less intact except for the living room, which was soaked with rainwater that had come through the damaged roof.

As I walked around assessing the damages, one thing struck me powerfully: no flood water was in any of the buildings. What a miracle! The church is built a few feet above the ground. But all other buildings were close to the ground, yet no floodwater seemed to be in any of them. Later I came to learn that we were in one of the few small "islands" in the whole area that was untouched by the floodwater. Almost 95 percent of the city was under dark, muddy floodwaters, but somehow we were spared!

Next I walked over to the church van that was parked on the side of the school building. I had never appreciated the van before, as this fifteen-passenger 1995 Ford van had given us plenty of trouble in terms of repairs and maintenance. My experience driving this van, or for that matter any vehicle larger than a car, was next to none. The only time I had driven it was a week prior to the storm when my car was at the dealership for servicing. On this day I found the key to the van in the parish office and cranked it up. After its usual initial hesitation, it started. I wanted to cry right there! "Lord, I love You, and I love this van too." But there was no way to get the van back to the seminary because the roads were cluttered with trees, downed power lines, and debris.

I walked as far as possible and found a few people on the road or by their homes. It was a joy to see another person alive, whether I knew the person before or not. We were all in the same shape—looking dirty, tired, and shabby. Simply the sight of another human person alive seemed to be the most important thing. Life! Life is precious, and we could appreciate its value even more after having survived a life threatening experience.

When I came back to the seminary and announced that we had a van that worked, it was a relief for all. All the cars at the seminary had gone under water, crippling our mobility. We were also faced with the health issues of some of our senior priests. It was going to be extremely painful for the elderly ones to remain in that situation. Some had rather bad heart conditions, one was a diabetic, and one of them was undergoing dialysis three times a week. Fr. George Artis, who was undergoing dialysis, was our main concern, and he looked weaker with each passing hour. We went by the Hancock Medical Center in Bay St. Louis only to be told that all the hospital equipment had gone under water.

We had seen helicopters by then, flying overhead actively engaged in search and rescue activities. A few of us ran to the soccer field next to the seminary and started waving frantically at them. God makes a way when there seems to be no way! To our amazement, one of the helicopters slowly descended, and we related the serious nature of Fr. George's condition. They graciously agreed to transport him to a health facility. Later we found out that he was taken to Mobile, Alabama, where he received his treatment and later was transported to Holy Ghost Church, an SVD parish in Opelousas, Louisiana. God works in mysterious ways!

Mike Benvenutti, a local business owner who had sold the generator to the seminary, reached us as soon as possible and got the generator running. After a couple of nights of total darkness, we appreciated the light. We also were grateful for the good food prepared lovingly by Ms. Elmira Farve, the cook at the seminary who, with her family, prepared meals in the days and weeks ahead.

One of the best and most practical things that people who remained in the community did was to clear the roads for vehicles to pass. At least one lane of all major streets was cleared. This allowed relief agencies and volunteers to have access to the community. We did our share of cleaning and were finally able to drive the van to the seminary.

Getting the rest of our retired priests to a healthy environment was imperative. We were so blessed to have a van in running condition. Fr. Jim Pawlicki and I volunteered to drive the priests to north Mississippi. The van had only half a tank of gas, but we thought gas would be available somewhere along the way. Since phones were not working, we had no idea that the storm had caused substantial damage to most of the northern part of Mississippi as well.

The communication systems were not working due to downed cell towers; therefore, we were unable to contact our SVD brothers in northern Mississippi to alert them of our condition or of our proposed trip. Several times I thought about my family back in India. How anxious my parents, siblings, relatives, and friends must have been! I was told later that they were very anxious and that prayer was the only force that gave them comfort and strength. Only when we traveled outside of Biloxi were we able to get a signal on our cell phone; then we could finally let the world know that we were alive and had survived the monstrous storm!

Our first stop was to drop off the older couple and the Chinese exchange student near Pascagoula, Mississippi. During the next leg of our trek, I saw tremendous composure and understanding from our senior priests. None of them ever uttered a word of complaint but were grateful for our efforts to get them to a place of comfort. Finally, we reached Meridian, Mississippi, but did not find our priest there as we expected. The sporadic cell phone reception had made it impossible to communicate clearly. Our decision was to proceed, hoping to find a gas station somewhere along the way. I recall constantly looking at the gas gauge as it neared the red zone.

We were exhausted from having little sleep in four days; we were hungry and thirsty, having just a couple of bottles of water among us. Finally, we came over an overpass in Chunky, Mississippi, and pulled onto a bridge to see if we could get any cell signal. No cell bars were displayed on my phone, but to this day I believe divine intervention allowed me to contact my classmate, Fr. Jaison in Baton Rouge, Louisiana, who was so excited to hear my voice. I could hear him screaming, "Man, where are you?" After giving him our whereabouts, I asked him for three things: to notify my family as soon as possible to let them know I had survived because they would be worried to death; to meet me the following day at St. Augustine seminary with gas, water, food, and help; and to alert Fr. Charles Boykens, SVD, pastor of St. Mary's Church in Vicksburg, Mississippi, that we were on our way and in need of food and supplies.

While we were waiting on the side of the road, Fr. Pawlicki was able to contact Fr. Boykens and describe our situation. He assured us he would meet us there as quickly as possible. We waited, exhausted. I witnessed the senior priests taking different medications, one having to inject insulin for diabetes. Some of them fell asleep. At one point, Fr. Theriault's sister, Marie Cyr (she was riding out the storm at the seminary and later found out her home in Pass Christian had been destroyed), woke up from sleep and remembered that she had two bananas in her bag and asked me to get them. But Fr. Pawlicki and I had come across them when we were looking for flashlights and had eaten them already. They were the best bananas I can recall ever eating. It did not feel sinful to eat them . . . until she asked for them.

Fr. Charles Boykens and one of his parishioners arrived at Chunky about 2:30 a.m. with gasoline, water, and snacks. We had not eaten anything since 12:00 noon on Wednesday. Even the water tasted delicious as well as the snacks. We spent the early morning hours in Vicksburg. The hot shower was so refreshing and I knew it would be several days or weeks before I would experience such luxury again. Fr. Pawlicki and I returned to Bay St. Louis the following day.

CHAPTER 6

Celebration of the Teary Eyes

On Friday, September 2nd, I received word that the Bishop of Biloxi, the Most Rev. Thomas Rodi (currently the Archbishop of Mobile), would be coming to St. Rose to celebrate the Mass on Sunday. Most of the Catholic churches along the Coast were totally destroyed or severely damaged. Those included our neighboring churches: Our Lady of the Gulf in Bay St. Louis, St. Clare's in Waveland, St. Ann's and St. Joseph in Clermont Harbor, St. Joseph Chapel in Cedar Point, St. Joseph in Pearlington, and St. Augustine Seminary Chapel. St. Rose was the only place in the area that could hold a service inside.

I felt that it was important to get the word out to as many people as possible. I rode around in the church van and tried to tell everyone I met about the Mass on Sunday and invited all to come. All were welcomed without any distinction of church membership or denomination.

I also felt cleaning the church and the campus that surrounded it was imperative to give people a sense of hope. I was able to gather some parishioners together, and we began cleaning the church. More people joined by the end of the day. By Saturday, we had cleaned the church, cut down some of the fallen trees, and removed most of the debris from the yard and the streets.

The Mass was an emotional experience filled with tears of joy and sadness. Joy came in spotting a friend and knowing that he or she survived. Great sorrow accompanied the shared rumors about the death toll. The official count, issued several months after the storm, estimated that 168 people along the Gulf Coast died in Hurricane Katrina. Our choir began by singing, "Encourage my soul . . . The storm is passing over" and thus began the "Celebration of the Teary Eyes."

The words of Bishop Rodi were of great comfort and encouragement. Every face in the congregation was soaked in tears. Quoting the classic text of Job's suffering from the Bible, the Bishop invited the people to put trust in the Lord, who alone has the power to know why certain things happen. I remember the following words vividly even today, "Tragedies can do two things to our hearts. Either they can make us bitter and our hearts stony hard; or they can make us better, our hearts mellowed with love and hope."

It was interesting to hear the bishop say, "I thank Fr. Sebastian, your pastor. He could have left this area and gone to a safe place with any of the parishes staffed by the Society of the Divine Word. I thank him for his decision to be with you."

I was asking myself, *Did I have a choice?* Even if I had succeeded in getting to Baton Rouge before the storm, I would have returned at the next available opportunity. In fact, I had already thanked God several times for allowing me to fail when I had attempted to evacuate, as my presence in some small ways brought some relief to people, specifically to the retired priests at the seminary. More than that, I would rather be in no other place than with the people of this wonderful community who had become my family. At this moment, they needed me more than ever, and I was not going to leave my people.

At the end of the Mass the bishop said, "I had the option of bringing all items for the normal celebration of Masses by the bishop in parishes, such as the shepherd staff and the miter. But I chose to bring you some water and other emergency supplies instead." That indicated to me right from the start that Bishop Rodi was committed to the process of recovery.

At the end of the Mass, we all stood outside for hours. Nobody was in a hurry; in fact, many had no place to go. Through tears and hugs, we assured each other of our support for one another and resolved that together we would survive this ordeal. Standing on that holy ground of the church, I knew God would make a way for better days in the future. Parts of the Mass and the gathering after the Mass were televised through national news media (Fox News), which brought St. Rose to the attention of many people. Several people who had evacuated told me how grateful they were to know that our little church had survived.

I distributed most of the items the bishop had brought right then and there. I took anything left into the school buildings. Something told me that I needed to clean the school building as soon as possible.

God works mysteriously. The powerful word in Isaiah was proven true, "Before they call, I will answer; while they are yet speaking; I will hearken to them" (Isaiah 65:24). My classmate, Fr. Jaison, visited St. Augustine on Sunday after the Masses, bringing more food, water, gasoline, and other items. He assured me that he had already spoken to his youth group and the youth advisors about their trip to the Bay on Monday, as it was Labor Day. They would come and clean up wherever needed. What an offer! I told him about the school building, and we went over there. He told me, "Consider it done." He called one of the youth advisors in his parish who owns a janitorial business and asked her to get all the supplies needed to clean up the school buildings.

Fr. Jaison kept his promise, and he arrived along with twenty young people and half a dozen adults from St. Paul's Church, Baton Rouge, Louisiana. They were willing to do whatever I asked of them. I could see from their faces that they were in shock after seeing the level of destruction all around them. After I briefly described my harrowing experiences during and since the storm, we got to work.

Later when we took a short break, we all went into the church and prayed. The children and adults had lots of questions about the storm. When I told them about the flood that had drowned over 95 percent of the Bay St. Louis and Waveland area, they were amazed. And when I told them that all of the buildings at St. Rose were unaffected by the floodwaters, I could see expressions of disbelief on their faces. Three to five feet of water was in homes and buildings right down the street, but not a drop of floodwater in any of the buildings of St. Rose! There was no logical explanation for it. No one could give a satisfactory answer to how that could have happened. I had the only answer possible—it was a miracle to behold!

We worked throughout the afternoon—cleaning up broken glass, rearranging and readying classrooms to house people from the area who were now homeless, clearing a large space in the school building, and removing debris around the outside of St. Rose. This little group of apostles was committed to their mission of helping others, and we would soon experience the next miracle.

In the late afternoon, a gentleman from Chicago, driving a pickup truck with a trailer, stopped at St. Rose because he saw the youth and adults cleaning up the school yard. He told us he and his three sons were so distressed by the news reports of

Katrina that they had loaded up supplies and headed to Mississippi to be of assistance. They had been driving around looking for people that needed their supplies. They had given out some things to people they had found at different places. The man seemed to be very impressed with the work we had already done, especially with cleaning the school and the yard. He said we were the only ones that he had found working. Everyone else seemed to be in a daze, overwhelmed by the enormity of the destruction. He then took out his wallet and pulled out a bunch of bills and put them in my hands, saying, "Use it any way you choose." The money was given to him by his pastor. It was about three thousand dollars, the first monetary contribution, but surely not the last.

When one has witnessed a miracle in life, the experience is not to be kept to oneself; it's meant to be shared. I had to pray ceaselessly to find an answer as to why, when practically every large building in the area was totally or partially destroyed, our buildings were spared. I came to the conclusion that God wanted us to make good use of this opportunity to provide every possible assistance to the recovery of the area. I believed that this place could become a beacon of hope for many.

When I returned to the seminary that evening, I joined others who were sitting outside and recounting the events of the day. I was told that some people were looking for me. It turned out that they were a group of people who had driven from Florida, bringing supplies. Wow! We had just finished cleaning up the school and people were already bringing things to us. The wonderful folks from Orlando, Florida, had decided to have a neighborhood gathering, requesting people to bring useful items for those who had lost everything in the storm. I led them to the school. It was amazing to see that they already had a plan to arrange items in an orderly manner. It was already

8:00 p.m., and they had a long drive back to Orlando, Florida. They were not even bothered with the time. They placed labels on the wall and separated all the different items under each label. I started learning from them about how to arrange things in the future when more donations were brought in!

It had been a day filled with miracles about the greatness of God and the spirit of humankind: the help of Fr. Jaison and his group of volunteers from St. Paul's Church, the generosity of the pastor from Chicago who had sent funds through the gentleman and his sons, and the blessings of essential supplies and organizational skills of generous neighbors in Florida. We saw that St. Rose was spared from destruction to be a beacon of hope for our community. All of these became fundamental lessons that I would draw on in the days and years to come.

CHAPTER 7

The Task Force

"There is method to one's madness" is an often used idiom when describing what looks like strange actions that are actually carefully planned ones. But looking back to where we were and how far we have come, I cannot claim that we had a perfect plan in place to make those things happen. Some procedures were in place to prepare for the storm, but there were no serious strategies for the aftermath of a storm. We made up plans as we went along. I can honestly say we reacted to circumstances more than we were proactive. When situations presented themselves, we responded to them. When opportunities presented themselves, we seized them and made the best out of them.

I knew it was important to share as much of the responsibility as we could with people who were willing to shoulder them. Most of those who had stayed behind had nowhere to go as their homes were either destroyed or severely damaged, making them impossible for habitation without serious repairs. Many were living in tents or had accepted the generosity of other family members or friends. Many had lost their places of employment. So on the second Sunday after the storm, I asked as many people as possible to linger for a short meeting after the Mass.

People stayed and shared their stories. We cried together, laughed together, prayed together, and assured our help for one another in days to come. We decided to meet together every week to catch up on things and to give information about the whereabouts of people and share where any forms of relief were available. This weekly meeting resulted in the formation of the St. Rose Hurricane Task Force. Since one of our parishioners (who is very meticulous and pays attention to details) was taking down notes, Bruce Northridge became the secretary of the meetings and eventually the chair of the Task Force, which would be later known as SOAR—the St. Rose Outreach and Recovery program.

In the first gathering, I requested that the parishioners volunteer to organize supplies that were arriving through the generosity and thoughtfulness of people from all across the country. We were receiving truckloads of water, food, cleaning supplies, clothes, personal care items, toiletries, and household items, all being unloaded into a ten thousand square foot area at the front school building. It began to look like a supermarket! All were welcome to shop for free at the St. Rose Relief Center. You name it and we had it right there, or we had the possibility of obtaining it. Hundreds of people came from all around to benefit from the available goods. A sign posted on the Center's wall said it beautifully, "For the Needy, Not the Greedy!"

Many volunteers from St. Rose and the Bay-Waveland communities worked diligently in the weeks and months to come to organize the items for the people of our area. The commitment shown by parishioners led by Beverly Williams, Donna Ellis, Marilyn Smith, Clementine Williams, Melinda Richard, Manuelita Curry, Jerald Jackson, Mary Coyne, Bruce

Northridge, Tamera Whavers, Carolyn Williams, Bill McIntyre, Nat Fairconnetue, Andrew Nash, Charles Johnson, Evelyn Curry, Marion Labat, Chari Lee, and others was absolutely outstanding.

Suffering and pain are compounded if people choose to be silent and do nothing to alleviate it. The good news was that from across the country, good people let us know that they shared our pain and suffering. They were not silent, but rather came to help and/or exhibited amazing words of encouragement through their letters, notes, cards, and poster boards. They offered prayers on our behalf. Some donated items that were vitally needed; some contributed generous amounts of money; others volunteered countless hours—all demonstrations of the greatness of the human spirit at work. For those of us who were on the receiving end, they were truly miraculous moments— God choosing to act through people.

Our decision to have a weekly meeting became very beneficial in many ways. Those meetings became occasions for people to share their stories, distribute information about available sources of help, pass out different forms made available by governmental and nonprofit organizations, get to know the whereabouts of the parishioners and members of the community who were displaced throughout the country, and plan our course of action for the weeks and months ahead. Sometimes we invited speakers from different organizations and agencies to provide information about filling out applications for FEMA or to answer questions concerning insurance issues, health support, and legal aid. Some of the meetings were attended by hundreds of people, while others were attended by a few dozen. Still other meetings were more intimate with just a handful. The tremendous camaraderie that we shared and the support we experienced from one another will never be forgotten.

The minutes taken at each of those meetings were distributed at the following ones and eventually passed on to others via email. When I went back to read those valuable records, I could not believe the number of actions that we were able to accomplish together. The decisions that had to be made quickly, the opportunities that had to be seized immediately, the deadlines that had to be met, the arrangements that had to be made, the items that were to be distributed, the volunteers who were to be housed, and all the work that had to be done looked very overwhelming. How did we do it all? Surely the hand of the Lord was working at a faster pace. He used many to be His instruments in this whole effort.

This pattern of weekly meetings continued for the first two years. Eventually we began to schedule meetings every two weeks, then three weeks, then four weeks. We developed structure as we went along. As more and more people played specific roles such as on-site coordinator (Beau Saccoccia), contractors (Brian Treffeisen, Nicole Pulkkinen, Rick Rechtien, Scott Kuhn, Kathy Litchfield, Jim Miller, and Sam Fletcher), kitchen coordinator (Loretta Treffeisen), volunteer coordinators (Jennifer Feltner and Molly Dugan), unskilled labor coordinator (Dee Salas), office staff (Marion Martin, Heather Bowman, Ashley Bowman, Morgan Lambert, Becca Rich, and Elaine Maxion), and executive director (Di Fillhart), the reports became more organized just like the work we were doing.

CHAPTER 8

Heaven Bestows Blessings

The first group of workers who helped to clean the church and grounds for the first Mass was St. Rose parishioners. Then the energetic youth group from St. Paul's Church in Baton Rouge cleaned the school buildings, which eventually became our shelter and distribution center. At that time I was not ready for the surge of people who would come to St. Rose as volunteers from all over the country in the weeks, months, and years that followed.

The relief center was going great. Many people came to share in the benefit of the blessings that were bestowed upon us by the people of goodwill from all around the country. Those items were stored in the front school building, which was about ten thousand square feet. We used the classrooms, hallway, and cafeteria to arrange items for distribution. A few families had taken shelter in the six classrooms of our back school building that had about six thousand square feet. We used these classrooms initially as shelter for people in the community; eventually they became the dormitory for hundreds of volunteers. We quickly constructed a Laundromat and showers in our outdoor pavilion.

The next volunteers who came to St. Rose were three men from New York. They said they were getting ready to go to Florida for a deep sea fishing trip when the storm hit the Gulf Coast. They decided to use the time they had set aside for their relaxation to come and help those of us in need. These wonderful men parked their trailer behind the school and made themselves available to be of service to the community in many different ways. They helped people put blue tarps on their roofs, they cut trees off rooftops, and they cleared debris. They were willing to do anything. Before leaving the area, they commented that this experience was much more meaningful and profound than any vacation they'd ever had before. They promised to share their story with others up North and tell of the resiliency of the people in our area as well as the many needs of the community.

No doubt each passing day was painful and joyful at the same time. It was painful because all around us were signs of destruction and loss. It was at the same time joyful because with each passing day we began to see little signs of hope for better days through the outpouring of volunteers and groups who came down to the area looking for ways to help. Volunteers gravitated towards St. Rose because we had plenty of space for them to pitch their tents; we readily welcomed them to become part of St. Rose.

A number of church groups and relief organizations, such as Calvary Chapel, City Team Ministries, Foursquare Church, and many others settled in Bay St. Louis-Waveland to provide nourishment and emergency assistance to the people. No barriers were between groups, and we were committed to working in collaboration with one another.

In one of the Task Force meetings, we discussed devising a needs assessment form. Oh boy, we did not know what we were getting into! Our first needs assessment form was simple: "What are your needs?" Was that not a stupid question to ask people who had just lost practically everything? The answers were overwhelming, as they ranged from immediate needs such as water, food, cleaning supplies, to household items, major appliances, money, and jobs. Other needs included cleaning, gutting, and repairing homes, and removing trees. Some wanted new homes. Many of those needs seemed impossible to meet during those early days, but they were legitimate needs.

I know that I serve an awesome God with whom all things are possible. However, for me to look at all the needs that people placed before me was overwhelming. I remember sitting down one night in my office, with both my hands over my face, just trying to fathom what was happening. I did not even realize at first that I was crying in my heart, and tears were trickling down between my fingers. This was the first time that I can recall crying in my adult life. I always thought that I had my emotions under control and could face any situation. Yes, I needed that cry—those feelings of helplessness and those emotions of inadequacy were more than I could handle. It was also a moment I realized that I was relying too much on my own strength, my own abilities, and my own planning. *Where is my trust in God for whom everything is possible?* I asked myself. It was a humbling and purifying experience, one that taught me that the work that I have been involved in was not mine but His.

That gave me a new perception. I know things do not happen with a snap of your fingers. God often does not accomplish things in life instantly. God uses people, events, circumstances, trials, and experiences to fulfill His purposes. God can use anyone, even those whom we might think unlikely. He also uses situations, events, circumstances, and experiences that we might consider irrelevant. The beauty is that God can use even people who do not know that He is using them.

Everything around us was overwhelming. But at the same time, the situation also put great opportunities in front of me. Once I was able to overcome my own thinking that I could handle these trials on my own and I realized I needed the help and support of others, things began to change in my life. When people called and asked what we needed, I had no hesitation in voicing the needs of the people, which until then seemed unrealistic. God was acting powerfully through people and situations, and what I needed was to put my trust and faith in Him. I knew that I was not asking anything for my own greed or for my own comfort, but I was being the spokesperson for people who were in pain. When people expressed their willingness to come down and volunteer their time in any capacity that I deemed appropriate, I had no hesitation in saying yes.

I received a call from Bob Coyne, from Silver Spring, Maryland, asking what he should bring when he came down to the area. I had no hesitation in saying, "Tools and cleaning supplies." He asked if there was anything special that I was looking for. My answer was, "Chainsaws." In a couple of days, he arrived with his daughter, Megan, in a pickup truck loaded with ten brand new chainsaws, work gloves, and tons of other tools and cleaning materials. He and several other goodhearted people provided us with much-needed tools to begin removing debris and cutting trees, and thus we began the St. Rose Tool Loaning Program. Families could sign out tools to do certain work and bring them back. As expected, some of them never came back, and I came to accept the fact that people might have needed them, so they kept them. However, most tools were returned.

I received another call from the Reynolds Family, who owned a trucking business in Pennsylvania, asking the same question, "What do you need?" This time my response was, "Building materials, particularly plywood and two-by-fours."

Within days, the Reynolds family arrived with an eighteen wheeler filled with all the materials we requested. Their church parish (St. Rose, North Wales, Pennsylvania) specifically solicited those items for us, and they responded compassionately to our plea.

When some young computer savvy volunteers arrived, I had no hesitation in asking them to set up computers with Internet connections and printers so our people could contact family members or access governmental forms to obtain assistance. Our computer café became a great source of help for hundreds of individuals connecting us to the outside world.

Learning to be receivers was difficult for many people. In many ways, we were all reduced to similar situations of helplessness. For some, they had to deal with their pride before saying yes to the help that was offered. Some felt that other people were worse off than themselves, and they were so gracious in expressing their concern that they might be depriving someone else who needed the help more than they. At times I felt that I had to convince people that they deserved the help, that they were not depriving anyone, and that enough help was available for all.

CHAPTER 9

Rising to the Occasion

Everyone on the Gulf Coast was touched by the kindness and goodness of people from all over the country. However, the role played by the faith-based organizations became the backbone of our recovery. The goodness of God shown through His people became the catalyst for transformation. Churches of all kinds arrived providing prayerful support, encouragement, and assistance to the communities of the Mississippi Gulf Coast. In the eyes of those who came to our aid, we were all the same whether we (or they) were Catholics or Protestants, Presbyterians or Methodists, Episcopalians or Church of God, Mormons or Baptists, Lutherans or Pentecostals, Mennonites or Quakers, Jewish or Buddhists, or nondenominational groups.

Although many of the local churches were entirely destroyed or heavily damaged, their congregations provided relief and recovery services to the Bay-Waveland communities and citizens of Hancock County. The notable efforts and works by Lagniappe Presbyterian Church, Powerhouse of Deliverance Church, Our Lady of the Gulf Catholic Church, St. Clare Catholic Church, Christ Episcopal Church, First Baptist Church, First Missionary Baptist Church, Valena C. Jones

Methodist Church, Lutheran Church of the Pines, Seventh Day Adventist, Word of Faith Church, First Presbyterian Church, St. Rose de Lima Catholic Church, and others are to be applauded. We were also touched by the kindness of the Buddhist and Jewish Communities, in particular Washington Hebrew Congregation and United Jewish Communities. The unity and oneness of the human family was evident in many ways as Carl Sandburg says so beautifully:

> There is only one man in the world
> And his name is All Men
> There is only one woman in the world
> And her name is All Women
> There is only one child in the world
> And the Child's name is All Children

Faith-based organizations such as the Salvation Army, Catholic Charities, Operation Blessings, Church World Services, and others such as Red Cross and AmeriCares served all who were in need. As a disciple of Christ, for me it was the Body of Christ coming together as one without distinction and division. Nuances of the first Christian community described in the Acts of the Apostles were at work in this situation of crisis: people who had shared with people who lost everything (see Acts 3:42-45).

Red Cross brought truckloads of supplies to our relief center on numerous occasions. From the earliest days, St. Rose had the privilege of working closely with the Salvation Army, which offered a multitude of services to the community. Catholic Charities brought a tremendous number of volunteers, building materials, and money to aid in our operation. AmeriCares became the single largest supporter in our rebuilding efforts by providing funds for building materials, major appliances, and covering some of the food expenses of the volunteers. Operation Blessings donated funds for emergency supplies. Church World Services helped us in restoring a few homes. The Fleming Journey Foundation from Houston was another reliable source of support in our efforts.

AARP helped our seniors with emergency supplies. This was made possible by Beth Labasky, whose parents, Craig and Marian Kergosien, are members of St. Rose. The Columbus Foundation in Ohio came in contact with us through Janet Callison (daughter of parishioners Carroll and Evie Gordon). This remarkable woman organized people of goodwill, raised funds through the sale of St. Rose Gospel CDs and other fundraisers, and became an integral part of our task-oriented work by sending down groups of volunteers at regular intervals. The amazing job done by the Habitat for Humanity group in Bay St. Louis and Waveland gave tremendous hope to many families, some who became homeowners for the first time.

St. Rose fortunately connected with many churches of different denominations and many different faith-based organizations. Some of them came to us due to individual connections, and some churches made the connection because we shared a common patron saint (St. Rose). Others came to us because the people who visited St. Rose were kind enough to spread the news about what we were doing, and some connections were made due to great efforts by the parishioners and leading community members. Some came to us due to the magnificent work undertaken by the diocese of Biloxi; others came through the work of the Catholic Extension Society; while others were brought to us by the providential hand of God.

I suspect even simple personal contacts probably left deep impressions about our community, which then became the catalyst for new relationships. A few weeks after the storm, we finally began getting sporadic reception on our phones, and I received a call from Fr. Tom McQuid of St. Leonard Church, Chicago, Illinois, which initiated a long-lasting relationship between the communities of St. Rose and St. Leonard. Fr. Tom had facilitated a week-long seminar for young SVD priests in Bay St. Louis in 2003, and he was thinking of us when the storm hit. Through another wonderful young SVD missionary, Fr. Adam McDonald, Fr. Tom was able to inquire about my condition and offered to help us through his parish.

The first people St. Leonard sent to our aid were a hard-working couple—Ron and Barbara Brohm. Soon they were embraced by our community, and they stayed with us for almost a month. Barbara helped in our relief center while Ron fixed things that needed to be repaired. The bathrooms that had detached from the church and collapsed on the ground were raised up, repaired, and reconnected with the church. Thank God that they are still standing! We set up a Laundromat with a few washers and dryers, which were in constant use for almost two years. As time went on, we had to set up signs that the Laundromat would close at 11:00 p.m! St. Leonard sent us generous donations at various times, and many wonderful volunteers came to work on various building projects.

A wonderful relationship between St. Rose and Holy Trinity of Washington, D.C. came about as a result of Leslie Conwell, the daughter of Lin and Jerald Jackson. Leslie and her husband, John, members of Holy Trinity, presented to their parish council a proposal to adopt St. Rose to help us get back on our feet. This wonderful community made substantial monetary contributions, sent down a great number of volunteers, organized several fundraisers, opened their homes to parishioners of St. Rose to visit or to live, adopted many families, and organized sporting events for the youth of St. Rose. They also sent down professionals such as lawyers, medical personnel, contractors, and teachers to help with different initiatives undertaken by St. Rose. Fr. Jim Shea, SJ (their former pastor) and Fr. Mark Horak, SJ (their current pastor) gave their wholehearted support to the initiatives their parishioners embraced.

The members of the Holy Trinity Task Force: Kathy Quinn, Margie Legowski, Frank and Norma Monahan, John and Ann Hisle, Maureen Leventhal, Richard Lash, John Bradshaw, Travis Brown, Sarah O'Neill, Rick and Marybeth Hendricks, Bob Reklaitis, and Grady Means were a few of the many wonderful people who planned and executed different activities between Holy Trinity and St. Rose. In my travel to this community to express my gratitude, they also provided opportunities to present our cause to concerned people in the White House (the Office of Faith-based Initiatives) and to the U.S. Bishops Conference (primarily members of the Catholic Charities and Extension Society).

St. Rose in Milton, Florida, also deserves a special mention of acknowledgment for their years of support to St. Rose. Fr. Dennis O'Brian and his parishioners made several trips to the Bay bringing items for the relief center and volunteers for rebuilding. Their monthly contributions that lasted for more than three years always seemed to arrive at the right time. I traveled to Milton with our well-known Gospel Choir, where they expressed our gratitude and performed at their annual church fair. The youth groups of both communities came together and had a great time of fellowship, prayer, and fun.

It was wonderful to see strangers becoming friends and our young people exposed to works of unity and togetherness. I was totally intrigued by the number of church communities bearing the name of St. Rose who wanted to support us: St. Rose,

Hazelhurst, Georgia; St. Rose, Hastings, Michigan; St. Rose, North Wales, Pennsylvania.

Prince of Peace parish in Taylors, South Carolina, was directed to us through the diocese of Biloxi. Knowing the good work that we were doing, the diocese informed this generous and giving parish about us. Jack and Pat Stewart were the first to arrive, assessing the situation before the parish made St. Rose a sister parish. The partnership that developed was wonderful. Several groups of hard-working people came down from this wonderful community of faith, and generous donations arrived from the parish and from parishioners over those four years. I traveled to this particular parish in 2007 to thank the people personally, to make known our ongoing need, and to celebrate Masses.

St. Francis of Assisi parish of Fairfield Glade, Tennessee, came in contact with St. Rose through the diocese of Biloxi. Though this community (largely retired) was unable to send any groups down, their generous monthly contributions made sure that we were able to continue our rebuilding work. Jack Smith, who had lived in Florida and had had his share of dealing with hurricanes, became a powerful voice for St. Rose in Fairfield Glade. I traveled to this wonderful community of faith and expressed our gratitude for their kindness.

Wilson Memorial Union Church, Watchung, New Jersey, came in contact with us through Kevin Northridge, the brother of Bruce Northridge, the St. Rose Peace and Justice Committee Chairman and Recovery Task Force Chairman. This New Jersey group made several mission trips and offered monetary help in our recovery efforts. The Big Canoe Chapel, Big Canoe, Georgia, was connected through Brandon, the cousin of Task Force member and parishioner Ames Kergosien. Their dedicated service and hard work impressed us all. St. Thomas More parish in Portland, Oregon, became our source of support due to Sue Gaden, a parishioner of St. Rose who had lost her beach-front home and relocated to Portland.

Fr. Bill Leon, full-time pastor and a National Guard chaplain, arrived a few weeks after Katrina. When he came to know about our recovery efforts, he offered the support of his church community, St. Anne's in Rochester, New York. St. John the Baptist Parish in Ottsville, Pennsylvania, also supported our efforts by sending down several groups of people and through generous donations. The Archdiocese of Milwaukee graciously offered us assistance by making two large financial contributions. St. Joseph Church in Prattville, Alabama; Immaculate Conception Church in Hawesville, Kentucky; St. Madeleine Church in High Springs, Florida; and Holy Redeemer Church in Odessa, Texas all became our partners through the work of the Catholic Extension Society.

If I were to write about each of the churches and what they have done for us, I'm sure many pages of this book could be dedicated to just that part of our story. The amazing grace of God was definitely at work through these churches and through their individual members. Indeed, faith was seen in action; love was shown through service; compassion was manifested through sharing our pain; and hope was kept alive through their kindness. Through it all, God was showing His face, His heart, His will, and His caring hands.

God was the One who made all things possible for us. In four and half years with the help of more than five thousand volunteers, SOAR worked on more than five hundred different projects. On three different occasions, St. Rose hosted more than three thousand volunteers from "Eight Days of Hope" (described later in the book) who worked on several hundred projects. Volunteers who came through Biloxi's Long Term

Recovery Committee and worked on projects initiated by St. Rose were many. At times the numbers get so confusing. The bottom line is that we became a conduit for God's blessings to flow to those who were most in need.

Our criterion for receiving help was simple. Most of the time, our efforts were directed to those who were most vulnerable in the community, starting with the elderly, disabled, single mothers, people with no insurance, people who fell through the cracks for whatever reason, and people who did not have adequate funds to repair and rebuild. Although the storm had reduced almost everyone to a precarious level of vulnerability initially, some were able to recover on their own or with very little help. The people of the Bay-Waveland communities will be forever grateful for the many selfless acts of assistance . . . and that help is what a countless number of churches and good-hearted individuals offered in our time of need.

Amazing stories of human resiliency, courage, and unity continue to shape the life of the Coast. The story of Ms. Eloise Thomas is one example that brings these beautiful qualities to focus. Recalling her experience of riding out the storm at her daughter's house, she says it was only faith in God that got her and her family through. She was forced up into an attic and later onto the roof to save her life along with other members of her family. Her limited mobility and the fact that she used a wheelchair were not major issues when it came to getting her out of harm's way. "God will see us through," she continuously assured her family.

The storm left her house severely damaged. It barely had a structure, and even that needed serious work and leveling. She prayed that something would come through. Yes, something came through in more ways than she ever hoped. The Haas family of Bay St. Louis, where Ms. Thomas had worked for many years, initiated an undertaking that was embraced by many people. I still remember visiting Ms. Thomas with Laura Haas and assuring her that we would get her back into her home. I was not at all sure how we would do it. Once again, God opened the doors of possibilities. Laura had knowledge of Washington Hebrew Congregations' willingness to help the victims of Katrina. The donation of fifty thousand dollars was offered to St. Rose with the understanding that the family's house would be restored and the remaining funds would be used for ongoing recovery needs.

We took up the project. Spearheading the actual work was Roger Stillman of the Lutheran faith from Florida. Rick Rechtien, who was working as a construction leader for St. Rose, worked on this house along with many wonderful AmeriCorps members. By the time we completed the house, there were people who were Baptists, Presbyterians, Methodists, Mennonites, Catholics, and many other groups who had contributed their significant share of work in this endeavor. This is but one of many stories where people belonging to all walks of life and religions and denominations (Jewish, Catholics, Lutherans, Baptists, Presbyterians, Methodists, Mennonites, and others) worked as one family to achieve a noble goal—bring a sense of normalcy back into the lives of people. This is a great testimony of what we can achieve when we are willing to put aside our differences and focus on the need at hand!

The Church—I mean the body of Christ and the people of faith—was like a bright light shining in the darkness. In a conversation with the acquisitions editor of Evergreen Press, I explained the topic of my book. He then recounted his experience during Katrina. He said he was riding out the storm in Mobile, Alabama, and he said he was praying for safety and protection when he clearly heard a voice say, "The Church will shine." He said he did not understand the meaning of the words then. Later he volunteered with his church community and came to Mississippi to help out with the recovery efforts. Seeing the initiative and involvement of the churches and faith-based organizations, he came to the full understanding of the words he had heard, "The Church will shine." Indeed, the Church did shine!

CHAPTER 10

Meetings, Meetings, and More Meetings!

I have attended numerous meetings in my life. I felt I had reached a point in my life (before the storm) where I could pick and choose those that I really wanted to attend. The constant of life is change; Katrina changed so many things, including my schedule. I have no recollection of the number of meetings that I attended after the storm. Some of those were called at St. Rose, but a vast majority of them were held in the larger community, organized by interfaith committees or at the diocesan level. Those were vital moments of information gathering and planning for better days. In many ways I was like a sponge, absorbing information and bringing the information back to the community. I remember making announcement after announcement about many opportunities that were available to people and about meetings that were taking place where people could get information firsthand.

Through these meetings, I was exposed to a great number of wonderful and dedicated people in the community and those who came from all over the country. The personal contacts that were established, the friendships that were formed, and the relationships that were fostered all were channeled into one thing—

to help the community get back to normalcy. I was honored to be part of the Governor's Commission for Rebuilding Hancock County. This gave me an opportunity to come closer to a large number of leaders in the community, and our appreciation for each other and the collaboration among us grew greater after that.

Of course as we can all sadly attest, we had our share of meetings that led us nowhere. Sometimes, people just talked and talked just to have their voices resonate across the room, resulting in no action. However, through it all, the goodness and wonderful intentions of the people were present.

We can always find reasons to blame others for our situation. I have done my share of that. Often, governmental agencies became the target of people's wrath and frustration. The amount of pain and suffering endured by so many was excessive; many felt that they had been abandoned. On the other hand, the magnitude of destruction was never really anticipated or planned for. The country (FEMA and other governmental agencies) was woefully unprepared for such a massive emergency situation.

Insurance companies quickly paid to homeowners the National Flood Insurance Program (NFIP) monies funded by the U.S. taxpayer. Most of the insurance companies—State Farm, USAA, Allstate, and others—entered into a wind versus water argument with policyholders, igniting people's fury for what was seen to be their poor and greedy handling of claims. Many homeowners who felt before that they were well-insured and financially protected in the case of a natural disaster were told otherwise—a bitter pill to swallow because they felt that their future and their security were being unjustly taken from them. Many legal challenges ensued and continue even today.

On the other hand, the local and state governments and the

law enforcement agencies in so many ways deserve special praise and appreciation for the magnificent work they undertook. They made the pain of the people known at a national level and received the necessary attention. The mayors of the two cities and councilmen (aldermen), Board of Supervisors, and law enforcement agencies rose to the occasion to meet the challenges. The leadership provided by Governor Haley Barbour and the senators was awesome. The tireless energy of our local Congressman, Gene Taylor, was contagious. They all had one goal in mind—bring the Coast back to normalcy.

Tish Williams led the Chamber of Commerce in keeping the plight of the people visible to other cities and towns while soliciting support to rebuild businesses and provide job opportunities. On the local level, committed leaders were involved in making things happen. They shared the same pain and were in the same plight as the rest of the community. Several prominent citizens put their personal recovery on hold and committed to working to bring the community back to normalcy. I cherished the opportunities to be in the same room or trailer with these committed members at our meetings, meetings, and more meetings.

CHAPTER 11

Sharing Gifts in 2005

God was moving powerfully in our midst. As Thanksgiving drew near, we made a decision at one of our Task Force meetings. It was very simple—give a fifty dollar check to every one of the four hundred families in the parish. Since we did not have the wherewithal to bring a Thanksgiving basket to every family, we felt St. Rose could bless its members with a small token of appreciation. We made no distinction here between rich and poor, as Katrina had reduced everyone to the same predicament in many ways. More than the amount, what touched the hearts of the people was the thought that the church community wanted everyone to have a bit more in this holiday season.

I remember a few people crying on my shoulder, overcome by this simple, thoughtful gesture. For a good number of people this was the first time they had ever received a monetary gift from the church. I said, "Think of it this way—all your life you supported the church. You took it seriously to financially support the church. I am sure you will continue to do so. Now the church, through the generosity of people around the country, is able to help you in your moment of difficulty." Some parishioners, though in bad shape themselves, wanted to give it to someone else who they thought was worse off than they were. It was a true season of sharing and seeking out the joy of others.

The holiday season was both painful and a blessing in many ways. Our phones kept ringing, primarily for two reasons. Many were calling to inquire about the assistance they could get from the church. An equal number of calls were about what kind of gifts people could bring to give to the people of the Gulf Coast. One offer was to provide a gift for every child in the schools of Hancock County. Initial plans were to provide a toy for every child. But somehow, the person who offered to spearhead the event was unable to pull things together.

By then we had made a promise to all the children through the newspapers, churches, and schools. Here we were! By then we had promised gifts to more than five hundred children. Somehow, we now had to keep our promises to them. Otherwise, children who had gone through so much deprivation and pain could once again feel that they were let down.

We were desperately thinking about solutions and ardently praying for answers. An idea struck me then to make our plight known to the parishes that had been supporting us as well as to the people in the parish through the weekly bulletin. We publicized that our goal was to give a gift card to every child for Christmas. In just a couple of weeks we received enough money to buy more than 750 gift cards of thirty to fifty dollars that we distributed to the children. I realized once again the great power of my almighty God. If we had let the temporary setback (the person being unable to pull things together) alter our decision, we would not have been able to bring a little more joy into the lives of more than 750 children.

Some of the children who received the gift cards and other gifts at Christmas wrote moving letters, thanking us for our efforts. In their little minds, we were the givers. Of course, we were not the givers; rather, we were just a conduit for God's blessings to flow to them.

Here are some testimonies from the children who received the gift cards:

"I didn't have any toys until I got the gift card. I am just writing this letter to thank all of you. I love my rocket that I bought. It goes six hundred feet in the air. I play with it every day. My brother and I love the rocket."

"Thank you for the thirty dollar gift card. I am going to buy a lot of stuff. You must have taken a lot of time to get them for all the children. Thank you for the trouble you did getting those cards."

"I like the gift card. I wanted thirty dollars and I got it. I really want to buy an Easy-Bake Oven or I could buy some silly CDs. I appreciate it. Thank you."

"Thank you for the gift card. I like it. We lost everything. I will buy some pants and a shirt with it. I am rich now."

"Thank you for the presents you gave me. I really liked it very much. I hope you come again next year."

"Thank you for the thirty dollar gift card. I had to give it to my cousin because he didn't get one and because he lost everything."

"Thank you for the gift card. I really like it. I can't wait to go shopping with it. I lost my house in the storm. I had seven feet of water. I lost all of my stuff in the storm."

"Thank you for the thirty dollar gift card you gave us. I am going to save it up until April, my birthday. Where do you live? Is it messy because of Katrina? Thank you for the toys and stuff you donated for the people who lost their homes."

"I appreciate the thirty dollars that you sent. I wonder how you got so much money to send to us. Thank you and have a Merry Christmas."

These simple yet heartfelt words were expressions of gratitude that were lingering in the air during those days. Everyone seemed to be excited about the holiday season despite their personal losses and enormous struggles. Many more gifts were still to come for people during the Christmas season of 2005!

Christmas arrives each year bringing the best gift to humanity in the person of Jesus Christ. For Christians, it is God's continuous act of love and mercy in the lives of His people. Human beings, despite their continuous rebellion, are never forgotten by God who, like a passionate lover, seeks to bring them back to His love. Christmas, therefore, is not just a remembrance of an historic event that happened two thousand years ago, but rather a visible manifestation of His love for us even today. When one goes beyond all the external celebrations that shadow the real meaning of Christmas, Jesus becomes the best gift God so lovingly bestows upon us. For me, Jesus came in 2005 in the forms of ordinary people who had extraordinary hearts and willingness to share their lives with us.

Sr. Florita Rodman, the administrator of St. Helen Catholic Church in Amory, Mississippi, came in contact with St. Rose through my fellow Divine Word Missionary priest, Fr. Gus Langenkamb, SVD. The wonderful community of St. Helen helped us in many ways. One of their important gifts was that they put us in contact with an amazing person—Steve Tybor, who was instrumental in bringing more than four thousand volunteers in their five trips to Bay St. Louis. His organization, known as Eight Days of Hope, embraced volunteers from all over the country and worked on hundreds of projects in Hancock and Harrison Counties. Their presence during the holidays and the hard work they put in were all reminders to us of a God "who loved the world so much that He sent His only Son . . . Not to condemn the world, but that the world might be saved through him" (John 3:16-17). This 2005 holiday season reminded us of God's love and mercy in this way: He loved us so much that He sent hundreds of good people our way!

These volunteers were not just people who worked on projects, but they were caring souls who set aside their time of relaxation to alleviate our pain. When they were not working on building projects, they were also in some ways soothing our aching souls. They did not merely bring presents for children at Christmas; rather, they brought hope into our lives. That was so visible when St. Rose organized a Christmas Party for all on December 16, 2005. Prayers were said, praises were sung, more than four hundred gifts were distributed to every child present that night, and we celebrated our hope as one family in the Lord. The smiles that were on the faces of hundreds of children were signs of the hope that was increasingly becoming a reality in the minds of the people.

This was also the time we became part of an "Adopt a Family" program. Hundreds of families who experienced loss were connected with hundreds of families elsewhere. Families could directly make their needs known to their partners and receive needed assistance for their recovery. Many of these blossomed into lasting friendships.

We also initiated a program called "Adopt-a-Child" to provide tuition assistance for children in private schools. This was very important as we did not want a family's post-Katrina financial strains to lead to decisions to take the children away from their familiar school environment. Of course, most of the school buildings were severely damaged or completely destroyed, and some of the teachers and students were displaced. It seemed important to retain as many children as possible in schools (whenever and under whatever conditions they reopened) so they could be in a healthier environment with their teachers and their friends.

An excerpt from St. Rose Newsletter describes how overall we ended the year 2005:

> Post-Katrina life remains a challenge on a daily basis. Most individuals and families at St. Rose and in the Bay-Waveland community are displaced residing in tents, temporary FEMA trailers, or with multiple families or neighbors in single-family dwellings that are in ill-repair. Many parishioners and residents have lost employment and health care benefits due to the destruction of local businesses. Access to health care remains very limited. Our local hospital was severely damaged due to the hurricane. Fortunately, the National Guard had set up a large M.A.S.H. unit, and doctors and nurses from across the U.S. provided immediate health care to residents of our county as well as to displaced persons from New Orleans. Recently, the hospital was able to reopen the emergency room but can only admit 26 patients to the facility. When the public school system reopened in November, only 39 percent of the post-Katrina stu-

dents returned, compared to 90 percent in Catholic schools.

Hancock County was reduced to ground zero. Of the four hundred plus local businesses, only 5 percent are of them are back in operation. The community is down to two operational gas stations, one grocery store, a couple of restaurants, one bank, and a few much needed hardware stores.

The rebuilding process is going to be a long and tedious endeavor. As the majority of our people have experienced considerable problems with their insurance companies and FEMA, a number of churches and faith-based organizations have shown the face of God, brought a spirit of hope to our people, empowering us to continue our journey of faith.

(from St. Rose Newsletter: *Spirit of Hope*—January 2006).

CHAPTER 12

A Tryout—House Repair

Our initial labor after the storm was to help folks in the Bay-Waveland area remove trees that had fallen on the roofs, put on blue tarps, clean out houses (aka "mucking"), remove debris, and clean yards to make room for FEMA trailers. We were able to accomplish this enormous task with the assistance of volunteers. However, I had no idea at that time that we would undertake an effort that would include repairing and restoring damaged homes and building new homes for the next four years.

Our prayer was, "God help us . . . and please send us some volunteers with construction skills." And of course, God heard our request and for the next four years, we built and repaired houses. Our test house belonged to Diane Frederick, who lived on Easterbrook Street, less than a mile away from the Gulf. The house was severely damaged so it was critical to get the roof fixed first before any interior work was initiated. A group of volunteers from Holy Trinity Catholic Church in Washington, D.C., and St. Leonard's Catholic Church in Berwyn, Illinois, arrived at St. Rose that week and in prior conversations had decided that they would take up the roof challenge with Travis

Brown of Holy Trinity as the project manager. It quickly became evident that we did not possess the right tools and/or skill set to get the job done. By the end of the week, we were exhausted, only had three-fourths of the roof completed, and the group held the record for the greatest number of trips in a single week to Lowe's.

Near the end of the week, the roofing crew sat outside St. Rose School one evening, reflecting on our accomplishment though still unfinished and strategizing how to improve our efforts. A revolutionary concept emerged, voiced by Chris Knauer, a member of the Holy Trinity Task Force from Arlington, Virginia. Chris suggested that St. Rose set definite weeks designated for a particular type of work and alert volunteer groups so that we and they could make preparations to accomplish the scope of work, obtain the necessary tools and materials, and stage them at the work sites. This simple, straightforward idea was the inspiration for numerous Roofing Weeks, Electrical Weeks, Dry Wall Weeks, and a defining moment that would shape our rebuilding efforts for the years to come.

The next day, we reviewed our needs assessment forms, identified several requests for new roofs, and selected eighteen based on their proximity and accessibility by vehicles. A couple of days later, Murray Chenevert, a contractor and parishioner at Fr. Jaison's parish in Baton Rouge, Louisiana, arrived. He and I set off to measure roof sizes and determine the volume of materials needed. From atop the roof, he would call out the numbers, and I would diligently write them down. At first, I had no idea what I was doing, but after a few houses I began to catch on and felt that I might have a new career as a contractor's assistant.

In January 2006, Bill Hefnago of Pittsburgh, Pennsylvania, called me to say he wanted to help and that he had extensive experience in construction. I told him of our roofing strategy, and he was filled with enthusiasm because this approach was music to his ears! Within days, Mr. Hefnago was in the Bay, examining the roofs, negotiating cost of supplies with vendors, and planning the Roofing Week. We held our first of many Roofing Weeks from February 19-25, 2006.

Simultaneously, several relief organizations in the community and at the diocesan level were attempting to partner long-term volunteer groups such as AmeriCorps and Hands On USA with local groups providing direct assistance to coastal residents who lacked the workforce to sustain such efforts. Surely, this described our situation at St. Rose, and I participated in several meetings to determine if we were a match. The stipulations were that if a group could provide food and shelter to the volunteer groups as well as building supplies and tools, then we would be an eligible partner. An air of enthusiasm surrounded the project, and we knew God would make it a reality, and He did—just in time for Roofing Week.

We purchased five sets of tools (compressors, nail guns, generators, etc.), which meant there could be five teams putting up five new roofs simultaneously. Several parishioners loaded up their pickup trucks with roofing materials and staged them at the designated houses under the direction of Bill Hefnago. Our amazing roofing teams consisted of more than sixty-five short-term volunteers from various churches across the country, long-term volunteers from AmeriCorps and Hands On USA, several volunteers from the Biloxi Diocese's Long-term Recovery Committee, and professional roofers from Hastings, Michigan. The preparation and cooperation were a great blessing. The work was hard and tedious, but there were no complaints, disagreements, or quarrels.

KaChunk! KaChunk! KaChunk! The sound of nail guns to shingles resounded throughout Bay St. Louis. By the end of the week, we had completed seventeen roofs—one short of our goal—and we choose to blame that one on the inclement weather! The following Monday, we not only completed the eighteenth roof but were able to repair one more, making our tally nineteen roofs and counting!

The professional roofers, calling themselves The Macquee Brothers, members of St. Rose Catholic Church in Hastings, Michigan, stayed on and completed five more roofs in five days. The St. Rose Roofing Week was a great achievement! It was a miracle in many ways, and it gave greater credibility to the building work being undertaken by St. Rose. Our success did not go unnoticed. Within a week, St. Rose-SOAR received fifty-two new requests for new roofs!

All the volunteers at Roofing Week touched our hearts in a very special way, and we were able to share our spirit of hope with them. Amazingly, four young volunteers decided to "pitch their tent" among us and work on building projects: Brian and Loretta Treffesien from New York; Jennifer Feltner from Holy Trinity Catholic Church, Washington D.C., and Beau Saccoccia, a Pass Christian native and recent Dartmouth graduate. Each assumed diverse responsibilities in the months and years that followed and most of all, they, by their example, taught us about love in action. St. Rose has been blessed by these and other wonderful people.

The success of Roofing Week empowered us to initiate several Electrical Weeks, Plumbing Weeks, and Drywall Weeks. Each of these weeks demanded the same rigorous planning, needs assessments, identifying funding sources for materials, ordering and staging materials, readying for volunteers, identifying project leaders, preparing and providing food and accommodations for volunteers, and securing permits. At times, obtaining permits and licenses seemed to be a great obstacle. However, I can honestly say that once the building departments realized the seriousness, professionalism, and legitimacy of our efforts, they were on board with us.

I cannot forget the generosity of Cote Electric Company from New Hampshire, who sent down four electricians and supplies to complete electrical work on several homes. I am also grateful to the Diocesan Long-term Recovery Office for funding Drywall Week, which eventually turned out to be Drywall Summer. I have never seen so many sheets of drywall or so much drywall dust in my entire life!

In between these specific goal-oriented weeks, several schools, colleges, church youth groups, and civic organizations came forward to help in our rebuilding projects. When we looked at our needs assessment forms, we found hundreds of requests for cutting trees, clearing debris, gutting homes, removing mold, and cleaning yards to make room for FEMA trailers. The needs seemed to be unending. The resources God made available were vast.

Many parishioners put their needs on hold to help with the work we had undertaken and managed the needs of the great influx of volunteers. I would like to commend the magnificent work done by parishioners Rhonda Labat, Marilyn Smith, Ames Kergosien, Gregory Farve, Lonnie Bradley, Paul and Florence Jordan, Manuelita Curry, Byron and Evelyn Curry, Andrew Nash, Marion Martin, Carolyn Williams, Bruce Northridge, Clementine Williams, Donna Ellis, Leatrice Cain, Jim and Jodi Beckham, Bill McIntyre, Racille McCullum, Mary Coyne, Peter Benvenutti, Sam Dorsey, Jerald Jackson, Mary Labat, Mark Kurka, James Kurka, and Phil and Beverly Williams.

The volunteers who came slept in the classrooms that were converted into dormitories. We constructed outdoor showers for them and never heard a complaint. Some classrooms contained more than twenty sleeping bags or cots. Many volunteers chose to stay in tents or in trailers. Several families accommodated volunteers in their homes. Many parish families volunteered to prepare delicious meals: Amy Kramer, Sunny and Candice Valentine, Alton Benoit, Charles Johnson, Raymond Collins, Tamera Whavers, the late Virginia Jones, Thyra Labat, Clementine Williams, Evie Gordon, Alvina Nichols, Goldie and Russell Fairconnetue, and Chris Lagarde are some names among many more. The pace was both exhausting and exhilarating! As one group of volunteers departed, I was grateful for the work done by Tina Harrell and Charlene Johnson to prepare for the next group of volunteers and make ready the "St. Rose Hotel."

In many ways our rebuilding efforts that contributed to the repair and restoration of hundreds of homes and building twelve new houses were successful because of the unity and hard work of many people—those who hailed from the community and those who arrived in our time of need. God was moving powerfully among us to restore hope and optimism in the hearts of our people.

Chapter 13

Exhibiting Our Frailties

I am not trying to paint a rosy picture about the situation after Katrina. In many ways, conditions were far from pretty. Even though we had amazing demonstrations of faith, human resiliency, courage, and sharing, many times our human vulnerabilities and frailties brought out the worst in us. Several times I sat down with people who voiced very difficult questions, which I found extremely painful to answer. Many of the questions were rooted in despair and frustration. People were not necessarily looking for answers but just wanted to be heard. And when they had a sympathetic ear to let their frustrations be heard, they often made the most of it.

"Why?" "Why us?" "Why do such things happen?" "I wouldn't wish this on anyone, but why couldn't this have gone elsewhere?" "Where is God?" "Why did He allow such a thing?" "How can there be so much destruction and evil?" "How will we ever recover?" These questions are very hard to answer in tragic times but specifically here with regard to what Katrina had brought. Some of the questions were asked with great pain, anger, or frustration. Nonetheless we do ask such questions.

Statements made in such difficult times can be more frightening than the questions. A statement often is the result of one's reflection and decision, depicting how one has chosen to deal with the situation at hand. I have listened with horror to these statements, "This is the end of my life," "I am giving up," "There is no God," "My future is over," "I will never make it," "I can't go on," and "I am going to die."

In my ministry I have had my share of dealing with situations that bring out these emotions. Often these are expressions of deeper realities. We all have a desire to be safe and secure. When the safety and security that we took for granted are unexpectedly taken away, we sometimes stumble and find ourselves uncertain as to how to deal with the reality at hand. The truth is that we all love our families, we love our homes, we love our communities, we all want security, and we desire safety. What we want is normalcy!

On many occasions I could not give answers to these questions or give words of wisdom to change their dispositions. I would sit down with them, be quiet, listen, maybe hold their hands or give them a shoulder to cry on. We would pray together, and I would assure them that better days were ahead. I would invite them to look at the blessings in life rather than the darkness. Most of all, I would challenge them not to limit God's power. Sometimes these words brought comfort to people, and sometimes they did not. People were usually gracious and they expressed gratitude for my time and empathy. But only time would tell if those moments we spent together would make any difference in their lives.

Dealing with people who are depressed and who have lost hope can sap one's energy. I found I was experiencing what the experts call "compassion fatigue." I thank God for the different organizations that recognized the mental health issues facing the community and created opportunities for people to vent. I thank God for the counsellors who were dealing with these situations. Sometimes, I felt it was more appropriate to direct some of the individuals in need to them, because I knew they needed more time and help than I could provide. However, one question would often linger in my mind, "Did I do enough for that person?"

This question came to mind in such situations because of an incident that I was reminded of frequently. It's a true story shared by one of my professors in a class I took on psychology and counseling. He said he was, at the time, counseling several individuals with drug and alcohol addictions. He was very concerned about one young man in particular. This man had a very strained relationship with the rest of his family. My professor seemed to be the only one in whom he trusted and confided. The professor said he used to receive phone calls from this young man several times a week. One of those phone calls came at 2:00 a.m. with the young man pleading for the professor to meet with him. The professor told him that he could meet with him in the morning and hung up the phone. The next morning he received a phone call from the family, informing him that the young man had committed suicide. Our professor told us he still blames himself for his decision to postpone the meeting. He believes that if he had made that sacrifice in those inconvenient hours of the morning, he could have saved the young man from killing himself.

There were more than a few conversations about people losing hope and talking about suicide in those days, weeks, and months after the storm. I felt the need to share a considerable amount of time with them. Sometimes it was meaningful, yet at times those sessions were very painful and burdensome. Sometimes I did not feel like being with anyone, let alone listen to another sad story. At times I felt impatience, irritation, and anger in my heart. At times I might have let insensitive and hurtful words escape my lips. Yes, I have had my share of brokenness.

In my years at St. Rose, people have been kind in complimenting me on my administrative skills. But even that taking-care-of-business mentality probably led to moments where my frailties revealed themselves. It's true in business that one tries to protect those resources that bring maximum returns. Maybe in my dealings with people who volunteered and who made donations, I may have exhibited greater appreciation and praise for those who came with the most volunteers or who donated the most money. I should have realized—especially as a priest—that it is not the size of the donations that mattered. What mattered was the good-heartedness and graciousness of everyone who came to help us, in whatever way that they were capable.

The vast majority of the people who came to our aid had only one thing on their minds—to help the families in the area. They used their time, skills, and resources to make a difference in the lives of many people. Some people came with good intentions and stayed on with mixed motives. Stories of contractor fraud were all around town. In some cases, people would receive their insurance money/grant money, and they would trust the contractors and pay them up front, trusting that their homes would be fixed. Aside from the rare case where the contractor would just skip town, the more frequent situation was that contractors would do a lousy job that would fail at the time of inspection. They would leave the homeowners with no money, and the contractors were either full of excuses or nowhere to be found. I remember sitting down with individuals who went through this experience, trying to comfort them and looking for resources to help them get back into their homes.

When you initiate an undertaking that involves people, it's

also clear that they bring with them both their gifts and their baggage. When you have an organization that became a conduit for more than five thousand volunteers to pass through, one has to expect the full spectrum of human experiences that include the good, the bad, and sometimes the ugly. I had my share of dealing with situations that were not so pleasant. There were disputes among volunteers, love-hate relationships, and unhealthy competition. Abuse of alcohol and a few instances of drug abuse happened. Through it all, we kept our eyes on the prize. We never let our attention be diverted by any of these isolated occurrences. These were seen to be small in comparison with the great good that was being accomplished by people who came with pure intentions.

One of the most intense moments of grieving since Katrina was the unexpected death of Dan Kivel, one of the volunteers from New York. This hardworking young man went wading in the waters of the Mississippi Sound just off the beach in Bay St. Louis. He was just relaxing and enjoying himself in the water after a hard week of work. The water seemed calm, but it unexpectedly caught Dan in a surprise rip current.

Immediately, a frantic search began. Then the authorities were called and we all searched for him for hours diligently, waiting anxiously to see what we feared had happened to him. His body was found after twenty-four hours. His death was a shock for all, causing great pain for everyone. Although I tried to remain strong for his team members, I felt a sense of anger along with grief in my heart. Why was this happening to this young man who came to offer his help and now had to lose his life? It was a time when my faith was challenged, and I did not have any answers at that moment.

Months later, we planted a live oak tree in front of the Holy Spirit Center in memory of Dan Kivel. The sprouting leaves and this new life reminded me, and remind all of us, that Dan still lives on, but in a different way. Our faith reminds us that the end of his life here on earth was, after all, the beginning of a life that will never end.

Occasionally the people who went through the pain and suffering brought on by Katrina also demonstrated their frailties. While great care and sharing was the norm, some people acted with greed and selfishness. On a few instances, the homeowners who received grants spent them on things that were not so wise. At times I heard comments from the volunteers that the able-bodied people in certain homes should come out and help. It was disheartening for the gracious volunteers to see some homeowners exhibiting lazy behavior when these volunteers had put their lives on hold to come to help people in need. Some were constantly looking for handouts without contributing anything from their end to better the situation. In retrospect, these were instances where our frailties and ingratitude were shown.

I would hear complaints from time to time about partiality shown to some and neglect shown to others. At times these complaints were directed against me. Here was an interesting paradox: some claimed that I was only helping people who belonged to St. Rose, while some asserted I was doing too much for people in the community who were not part of St. Rose. I often reminded myself of the need to remember that the good people from all over the country trusted me with their contributions. My challenge was to be a good steward of people's generosity by being the correct conduit for the blessings to flow to people who had the most need. People advised me as to how best to use the resources available, and I listened to them. Stories were also shared in confidence (by both donors and potential recipients) that people were unwilling to let anyone know about. That meant at times I had to make a decision based on my gut feeling. My prayer at those moments was for greater wisdom and discretion in making the right decision.

Sometimes my decisions were not the best, but those were moments of learning as well. Some families benefited more from St. Rose's Outreach ministry than others. The reality is that some of those who benefited were also those who worked hard for their community and continue to work hard for St. Rose. But at times I felt that my goodwill was being abused by some. At times I showed my own frailty when I lost patience with people and showed them my ugly side by not recognizing their needs. But in spite of all this, I could see God working in and through us. Often these situations of weakened spirits led to greater dialogue by which some were healed and troubles smoothed out, without causing perpetual damage to anyone's soul.

I felt a profound sense of gratitude to those who were willing to come and challenge me about some of my decisions. These were moments of grace in which we could clarify cases of misunderstanding at hand and move on with our lives. I also learned well that "You can please some of the people some of the time; but you can't please all of the people all the time." I knew if my intentions were to please people, I was in the wrong business. So my constant prayer was to please God at all times so I could please those who were in legitimate need.

Even though we knew that normalcy would not return to the Gulf Coast for a long time, none of us at St. Rose imagined that the work undertaken by St. Rose would go on until the end of 2009 (four and a half years). Besides the examples of our limitations, other factors such as the lack of facilities to house volunteers, dwindling donations, and a thinning volunteer force could have been valid reasons to abandon our recovery efforts. But the more we looked around and saw hundreds of families still in pain and suffering, the more we realized we just could not bring ourselves to shut down our operation. We trusted and believed that God would continue to provide and show us the way. And He just did that!

CHAPTER 14

Keeping the Spirit of Hope Alive!

Most of the national media coverage of Katrina focused (and continues to focus) on New Orleans and the horror and devastation they faced because of breaks in the levee system leading to massive flooding. That coverage led to the outpouring of assistance they received from volunteers nationwide. This wonderful city deserved every form of attention and disaster assistance available. Unfortunately, the Mississippi Gulf Coast, which experienced the eye of the storm, received far less national attention and assistance. For our part, we found various ways to communicate our story.

Initially, we communicated our desperate needs to friends and families across the country via phone conversations; and then they would spread the word to their neighbors, coworkers, communities, and churches. In response, we received thousands of calls letting us know that volunteers and supplies were on their way. We also received thousands of letters expressing concern and providing monetary donations and promises of prayers to support our relief efforts.

These acts of kindness deeply touched my soul, and I was committed to pen a personal note of gratitude to each one as soon as possible. I experienced a great sense of joy in being able to respond, for it helped me realize how very good people are. I found comfort in expressing our gratitude. While I was writing, parishioners helped out by addressing, stamping, and mailing our notes of thanksgiving. Words are not enough to express my gratitude to our St. Rose parish secretary, Chari Lee, as well as Marion Martin, Clementine Williams, Tamera Whavers, Manuelita Curry, Lili Stahler, Cookie Mittelbronn, Denise Prados, and many more for their assistance.

Volunteers who had returned home and people who had communicated with us by phone, letters, or email wanted to receive regular updates on the progress being made at St. Rose and the Bay-Waveland communities. In response, the Hurricane Task Force decided to issue the *Spirit of Hope,* a post-Katrina newsletter updating our supporters across the country on the latest recovery, rebuilding, and resiliency efforts at St. Rose. These newsletters became a powerful tool in communicating our story, of sharing our progress, expressing our needs, and requesting further assistance. The newsletters also served to acknowledge the many churches, organizations, and individuals across the country that were helping us.

The first newsletter was issued in January 2006, just four months after Katrina. In it I wrote the following:

> Just six days after Hurricane Katrina, St. Rose gathered to celebrate the Holy Eucharist with Bishop Thomas Rodi. Much had changed in the lives of parishioners and much remained the same. There were no lights in the church, no musical accompaniment, holes in the roof, and blown-in windows, but our tightly knit multiracial (and multi-denominational) congregation was there to give praise to the Lord. In the midst of the

raging storm and its aftermath, in the process of cleanups and rebuilding, we were continuing to seek peace. How long would it be before we reached some level of normalcy in our lives? Regardless if it would be eight years or fifteen years, we know that the St. Rose community will play a vital part in the rebuilding process.

Over the past four years, nine issues of the *Spirit of Hope* were published and mailed to our supporters. This was made possible by dedicated members of the Hurricane Task Force: Rhonda Labat, Mary Coyne, the late Susan Ross, Lili Stahler, Bruce Northridge, Marion Martin, Geoff and Sandy Belcher, Beau Saccoccia, Di Filhart, Fr. Jim Pawlicki, and many more.

When I look back I can say I did not anticipate all the work St. Rose would undertake to help the community on its way to recovery. That is why I come back to the source of my strength, God, who made it all possible.

I know that our human nature can have short memories when things are not right in front of us. We hear about tragedy and our hearts are moved by it, and we might do something to make a difference. If we have the opportunity to visit the place and see for ourselves firsthand the struggles of life, our support will be more enduring. But if we allow ourselves to walk a few steps in the shoes of a victim, our lives may undergo tremendous transformation.

We were blessed by the visits and involvement of many people who returned to tell our story to people they met. In October 2005, St. Rose was blessed with the presence of two permanent deacons: Art Miller and Tom Mack, who participated and spoke at our weekend Masses. Deacon Miller from the Archdiocese of Hartford, Connecticut, told the congregation that he was from one of the wealthiest states in the country but was returning home to tell the story of the true riches he found in Mississippi. Deacon Mack from the Diocese of Raleigh, North Carolina, told us that his story was witnessing how we were "blown into togetherness—not blown apart."

I'm not sure how much the St. Rose community was aware of the spirit of oneness and unity that was forever bonding us together as individuals and as a parish, and how much we were witnessing to those who volunteered or visited our area. We were growing as a parish, and we were learning to help and rely on one another in new ways—physically, emotionally, and spiritually. We were also learning what it means to be a church from the love in action taught to us by the volunteers. That witnessing was not just the work of human minds; for me that witnessing was the powerful work of the Spirit of God, who was moving mightily among us. When I look back, I know that God was radically transforming all of us.

CHAPTER 15

More Stress, Less Stuff, Yet More Joy!

The lives of survivors after a natural disaster go through cycles of ups and downs. Facing the reality that your familiar world has ended is a mind game that comes back to hound you again and again. At times one feels overwhelmed by the enormity of the challenges at hand. For some, the uncertainty about what lies ahead makes life all the more unbearable. Undergoing suffering is not a virtue at all, though it is likely to create some. Virtue is not about what happens to us but about what we do with it.

Stress becomes part of routine life, and people deal with it differently. Some search for quick answers, others find temporary relief in mind-altering substances or sensual pleasures, some wish to blame everyone else for their situation, and some blame themselves for their condition. Such attitudes can take away the ability to find meaning and purpose for living. Sometimes people just exist, not being fully alive. In those times, even a loved one can become a target of frustration and anger.

I know stories of how people drifted apart as a result of the storm. People who thought that they lived loving and caring lives before the storm found themselves fighting on a regular basis, affecting relationships within the family or extended family. Some hurt others because of their deep hurt within. Some families were ripped apart by the storm just as it had ripped apart the Gulf Coast. I have sat down with some of these people, trying to calm them down and help them to see beyond the immediacy of what is happening to them. Unfortunately, my efforts for some meant nothing, as they were too overwhelmed by the situation in which they found themselves. With pain in my heart I have watched people drift apart. My hope and prayer is that, with time, they will find healing and new direction.

I also witnessed instances where individuals and families with strained relationships or who were drifting apart found themselves coming together as a result of the storm. People have shared with me their stories where disagreements, quarrels, separation, and anger had severely damaged their family ties before the storm. I found one story in particular to be a very powerful moment of witnessing for me. In this family, each party had hurt the other, and each was blaming the other for his or her miserable condition. In their moments of anger, these family members only looked out for their individual well-being and did not care about what happened to the other one. But when the storm arrived and they were in two different homes, they both later admitted that they were praying for the safety of the other. Reconciliation was easier once they admitted what was important in life.

Situations of this sort can remind people of the many beautiful things of life and can bring into focus what is truly worthwhile as well as what is unimportant to them. I have come to know people who declare that they are better because of the storm. In no way were they saying that they loved the storm or the painful moments afterwards. Rather, they seemed to be saying that they have a newfound ability to look at life from a different, more positive perspective.

One of the amazing things that happened to people was a newly discovered realization of how precious life is. Having experienced the precariousness of human existence and fragility of life, they began seeing life in a new light. All who encountered that moment when death was staring them in their face soon realized that the most important prayer and hope in their hearts was to be alive! In the immediate time after the storm, the great joy was simply to see another person alive. Whether you knew them before mattered not; you were just joyful to be in the presence of another human being.

I have heard stories of people who talk about the purification that occurred in their lives as a result of Katrina. Material things and possessions that they worked hard to accumulate were painfully taken away. When they were able to come to the realization that they had lost just stuff they could live without, they felt a sense of liberation and freedom. Stuff no longer determined their happiness. Stuff didn't hold much meaning after you had faced death. You realize you can't take stuff with you when you are gone. You realize you do not live for stuff, and that stuff is only there to help you live comfortably. To realize that things do not need to determine your quality of life nor give you a sense of purpose was liberating for many.

In these painful moments, many found strength in their faith. This was not just the experience of the regular church-goers, but even those who had detached themselves from a body of believers for a long time found strength in their sometimes forgotten faith. Faith gave them a new direction. Faith enabled them to realize the strength of their character. Faith was the main catalyst for many people of goodwill to act the way they did. Faith enabled people to be kind, compassionate, and generous. "If not for our faith where would we be?" was a sentiment that was echoed by many—both victims of the storm and those who came to the aid of the victims. Many who came to be the givers also realized in their lives that they were actually showing their faith in action through their caring presence, dedicated service, and generous spirit. I suspect that this was the reason that many expressed clearly that "we received more than what we gave."

Some volunteers came to escape a painful situation or crisis in their own homes. Coming down and helping the recovery efforts provided beautiful therapy in their own lives. They looked around and found people who were joyful and decided to rebuild their lives in spite of all that they had been through. Often, the troubled ones realized the need to be grateful for the lives and situations they had. I remember a young person saying clearly, "I thought I had problems. Looking around here I know how blessed I am and at the same time how ungrateful I've been. I am a better person today because of what I saw here. Hopefully I will live a better and more grateful life." In simple terms, that person was going to be a better person, and his family was going to be a better family.

Yes, there was stress. Some of that stress led to unfortunate decisions and destructive choices. Yes, there were fewer things, and some things were smaller (compare a house to a FEMA trailer, for example). But through it all, we came to discover the bigger and better things in life. Yes, there were moments of anger and grief, but new realizations of the preciousness of life and the strength of our faith gave us a new joyful vision for life.

CHAPTER 16

First Anniversary

As we moved into the first hurricane season after the storm, a level of anxiety and stress was in everyone's heart. We were not even ready to hear about another hurricane season. But that is a reality that one has to face year after year here on the Mississippi Gulf Coast. As some might say, "That's the price you pay for living near the water." Thank God the season was a peaceful one, and we were soon nearing the first anniversary of Katrina (August 2006).

In so many ways the first anniversary of Katrina was emotional. Government officials made new promises about making the Coast stronger and more vibrant. The whole nation was reminded once again of the reality of how much more work still needed to be done. Ironically, many people who never saw the situation firsthand had come to a conclusion that conditions were more or less back to normal. The news media continued to focus on the precarious condition of survivors and how much still needed to be done. Although the limelight was still on New Orleans, people who were connected to Mississippi (and Hancock County in particular) still got the picture. A renewed enthusiasm was prevalent among the volunteers and donors to bring normalcy back to the Coast.

Various gatherings that were organized by the churches, cities, and organizations focused on two aspects: gratitude for how far we had come and hope for better days ahead. The St. Rose Gospel Choir performed at one of the services in Pass Christian, Mississippi, that was televised nationally. The whole gathering was so grateful for Robin Roberts of ABC, a local celebrity in the mainstream national media. We were all so proud for her and thankful for the unassuming and dedicated service she gave to the Gulf Coast. On a personal level and on behalf of St. Rose, we were greatly blessed by her dedication to the community and particularly to our children.

I was also part of several prayer services that took place in various locations. The gathering at St. Rose and the prayer service were both emotional and at the same time strengthening. We recalled the suffering the members of the community had endured; we remembered the people who died; we cried with people who were in pain; we expressed gratitude for every good thing God made possible; we hoped and prayed for better days ahead. The prayer of Archbishop Oscar Romero of El Salvador that I recited at the sunrise service on the beach captured the essence of our situation and recovery in so many ways:

> It helps now and then to step back and take the long view.
> The kingdom is not only beyond our efforts,
> It is even beyond our vision.
> We accomplish in our lifetime only a tiny fraction
> Of the magnificent enterprise that is God's work.
> Nothing we do is complete, which is another way of saying
> That the kingdom always lies beyond us.
> No statement says all that could be said.

No prayer fully expresses our faith.
No confession brings perfection, no pastoral visit
    brings wholeness.
This is what we are about:
We plants seeds that one day will grow.
We water seeds already planted,
Knowing that they hold future promise.
We lay foundations that will need further
    development.
We provide yeast that produces effects far beyond
    our capability.

We cannot do everything,
And there is a sense of liberation in realizing that.
This enables us to do something, and to do it very well.
It may be incomplete, but it is a beginning, a step
along the way,
An opportunity for the Lord's grace to enter and do
    the rest.
We may never see the end results,
But that is the difference
Between the master builder and the worker.
We are workers, not master builders,
Ministers, not messiahs.
We are prophets of a future not our own. Amen.

(This prayer was composed by Archbishop Oscar Romero, who was martyred in El Salvador in 1980.)

CHAPTER 17

Rebuilding the Church Buildings

The Catholic Diocese of Biloxi, spread across the lower sixteen counties of Mississippi, had more than one hundred buildings heavily damaged or destroyed as a result of Hurricane Katrina. The Diocese was not immune to insurance battles. The estimated damage was more than one hundred million dollars, while the insurance cap and reimbursement from the insurance company was limited to just thirty-five million dollars. That meant that only 35 percent of the total losses would be covered. This was a bitter pill to swallow for the Diocese and for the local churches.

Following the storm, St. Rose parish had some difficult decisions to make regarding the continuation of our Parish Center building project. Just five months earlier, we had broken ground for the Center, and after a rigorous capital campaign had 60 percent of the monies on hand towards the cost of the building, which was estimated to be about nine hundred thousand dollars. After Katrina, I could not, in good conscience, continue with the capital campaign and expect parishioners who had lost everything to be faithful to their pledges. After discussions with the Parish Council and Finance Committee, we decided to call off the campaign and delay our dream of a parish center, convinced that our greater responsibility was to help people rebuild their homes and lives. We trusted that God would help us. We did not know the details of how and when, but we knew God would not fail us.

In the *Spirit of Hope* newsletter, I informed our supporters of our dilemma of having no gathering place for parishioners and the people residing in the Bay-Waveland communities. All our public places were destroyed, and we had resorted to tent or outdoor meeting places. In one issue, I proposed that our half-built parish center, if completed, might meet this need. But I also made it clear that our first priority was to help individuals in need.

God answered our prayers in so many miraculous ways and far beyond what we ever imagined! First, our contractor, J.O. Collins, Incorporated, agreed to continue the work as soon as he could find workers while we searched for funds to pay for the center. Generous contributions started pouring in from across the country to support the completion of the parish center. What touched me the most was the response from my parishioners, many who had lost everything and yet gave a part (in some cases up to 10 percent) of the money they had obtained from their insurance settlements. The response was beyond our imagination and enabled us to commence once again with the construction of the parish center in December 2005.

We celebrated the opening of the new center on August 20, 2006. This was such a great achievement—not just for the parish, but for the whole county! The parish hall, named the "Holy Spirit Center" (to honor the memory of the Missionary Sisters of the Holy Spirit who served at St. Rose for more than seventy years) was the first large community building to be completed in the whole area. We shared our blessing with the larger community by hosting a variety of activities, such as public and civic meetings and relief organization meetings; for housing short-term volunteers; for wedding receptions and concerts for the community; for blood drives sponsored by the American Red Cross; and for Sunday Suppers sponsored by the Foundation for the Mid-South, a St. Rose resiliency program funded by the United Jewish Community that provided food, fun, and fellowship to residents of Hancock County.

In the meantime, the temporary repairs of the church were being done. It was a miracle that we never had to cancel any weekend Masses at our church. The wooden structure built in 1926 had not sustained serious structural damage. People were so willing to accommodate the inconveniences. When it rained, water poured into the church through the damaged roof, but people seemed to bear it with great graciousness. One of our supporters, Bob Glazer from Florida, had arrived at St. Rose and brought 250 gift baskets for the Thanksgiving holiday. He was in attendance at the 4:00 p.m. Mass on Saturday. The heavy rain that afternoon caused water to pour into the church from the damaged roof, soaking many who were in the church. When Bob returned to Florida, he gathered funds and sent us the money to repair the roof. Even the rain that was seen as a nuisance became a source of blessing for us.

Expressing thanksgiving to God through music is a high priority at St. Rose. Katrina had damaged our organ, piano, and sound system. Musicians from the Arizona Music Festival heard of our dilemma and dedicated the proceeds from one of their events to purchase a new electric piano for St. Rose.

Missy Treutel Schmidt, a former resident of Bay St. Louis came to know about our recovery efforts and needs at the church. She garnered the support of parents, fellow teachers, and children at Christ the King School to replace the damaged carpet throughout St. Rose. In addition, this amazing woman assisted families in finding temporary housing for people who had evacuated to Daphne, Alabama, after the storm.

Major restoration of the church had been put on hold until we could come up with enough funds to begin repairs. The community will remain most grateful for the generous donations of Frank Heath, Jr. and the late Leo Seal, Jr.

Our school building sustained storm damage, and it was critical that repairs be conducted promptly since its new purpose was to serve as a Relief and Distribution Center as well as a shelter for local residents and volunteers. World Vision, a nonprofit relief and development organization working with the poor and oppressed throughout the world, heard of our distress and responded to our needs through a generous charitable donation to repair the school for its new mission. St. Rose was fortunate to receive a donation from the Bush-Clinton Katrina Fund, an initiative undertaken by two former presidents. Yes, tragedies have a powerful way of bringing people together to alleviate the pain of the victims.

Prior to the storm, the rectory (which was in deplorable condition and infested with termites) was scheduled for demolition, and plans for a new rectory had been accepted by the Parish Council. Once again, Katrina changed our plans! The once-thought uninhabitable building looked better than many of the structures around town that were still standing. We converted the rectory into the SOAR Program Office and housing for long-term volunteers. In addition, we were able to purchase the house next door to serve as the new rectory because of the generous contribution of ten thousand dollars from Deacon Richard Turkot of Catholic Charities from the Archdiocese of Miami, and contributions from many other donors. Yes, God was moving in a mighty way!

Following Katrina, few places were available for children and adults to engage in recreational activities. Our new recreation was hunting for our lost treasures in piles of debris! Parishioners and residents were exhausted and had no respite. We were very concerned that if our teenagers had no fun and healthy activities to engage in that they might get into trouble. We were concerned that individuals and families living in FEMA trailers were becoming despondent. Parishioner, parent, and architect John Anderson and I discussed this problem and possible solutions. Our very ambitious goal was to create a recreational pavilion comprised of basketball and tennis courts next to our existing baseball field. This dream became a reality in 2008 and an opportunity to bring some fun back to the Bay! Clearly, God was making a way for us to play.

CHAPTER 18

SOAR: St. Rose Outreach and Recovery

By the end of 2006, the repairs of the school buildings were going full swing. St. Rose was renegotiating with the Mississippi Action for Progress to get the Head Start program back into its school building. However, this posed a dilemma for two reasons. Having Head Start was something the community truly needed. (Imagine being a young child living in a FEMA trailer for two years!) But having Head Start back in operation would also give St. Rose an additional income. To bring Head Start back meant losing the school to house volunteers for rebuilding. So many needs were still unmet—several hundred families on our list needed our help for decent housing, either by repairing, renovating, or by new construction.

We prayed about possible solutions to the dilemma. Mississippi Action for Progress made it clear that they wanted Head Start to be back in a permanent structure for the 2007 school year. One consideration for a short-term solution for housing volunteers was to find accommodation in the homes of people who had moved back. In fact, some families were already housing short-term volunteers in their homes from which lasting friendships were formed due to the hospitality and graciousness of homeowners in the community. However, I felt that with the large groups of volunteers we were receiving, the situation would become unmanageable. We thought about renting a few homes, but the cost and availability made that unrealistic.

Knowing the power of prayer, we continued to pray for a solution to this situation. In a conversation with Beau Saccoccia, who was volunteering with HandsOn Network and working on St. Rose projects, he made a suggestion about the potential of turning the William J. Kelley, SVD Retreat Center into a volunteer housing facility. I loved the idea for various reasons, and we decided to move in that direction.

The William J. Kelley Retreat Center, under the administration of the Society of the Divine Word, served as a place for prayer and retreats for hundreds of groups over many decades and has great historical significance. Originally it was part of St. Augustine seminary, built in 1924 to train African-American men for the priesthood and religious life. Due to the racial situation that existed in the country, African-American men were not admitted to any Catholic seminaries in the country. The Society of the Divine Word, an international religious order established in Germany in 1875, pioneered the development of indigenous clergy in the different countries where they worked. This brave initiative of the Society was implemented in, of all places, Mississippi in 1924!

Several decades later, the seminary was relocated to Chicago, Illinois, and the buildings were converted into a retreat center. Eventually the buildings were torn down and a new facility with five separate buildings was constructed in 2003. These buildings were severely damaged by Katrina floodwaters of six to eight feet. The buildings were adequately insured against wind and hail. Being located on one of the high grounds of the city, it was underinsured against flood, and 90 percent of the damages sustained were from the storm surge. The buildings had to be gutted out completely, carpets removed, electrical and plumbing works redone, floors laid, and walls painted.

This opportunity definitely seemed like an answer to our prayers. We experienced a moment in which God brought us an opportunity in answer to our prayers, and we had the choice to accept it or reject it. We said yes to the challenge, knowing that God would show us a way. The partnerships that were formed with HandsOn, AmeriCorps, Catholic Charities, The Salvation Army, AmeriCares, Gulf Coast Community Foundation, NAASC, City Teams Ministries, and various church groups and individuals were used wisely to repair the five buildings (over twenty-five thousand square feet). All parties benefited from this undertaking. Without adequate insurance coverage to restore the buildings, the Society received the free labor offered by St. Rose's collaborative efforts. St. Rose now had a building that could house over one hundred volunteers at a time for the next eighteen months!

As noted, we did not have a plan in the aftermath of Katrina. We were seizing the opportunities that God was bringing into our lives. It did not matter how it came, where it came from, or how it was made possible. We were all His instruments! I always believe that God can take what we have, which is often little, and turn that into something great. Our ordinary abilities coupled with His extraordinary power and grace can result in amazing results.

As we moved into the retreat center in January 2007, we also adapted a new name to our efforts: SOAR—St. Rose Outreach and Recovery. We were soaring at great heights because of the grace of God. He was the wind beneath our wings. He touched the hearts of many people to make this a reality. Over sixteen hundred volunteers were housed in these buildings in the next eighteen months, offering assistance to repair and rebuild hundreds of homes. On the same campus, we had SOAR, AmeriCorps, The Salvation Army, Catholic Charities, HandsOn Network, and others offering a multitude of services.

We began expanding to other services. The motto of SOAR was "Building a Stronger, Healthier Community." In addition to our building programs, we had health fairs, resiliency programs, and art programs for the youth and seniors. With a grant from Foundation for the Mid South, we had monthly Sunday Suppers that gave opportunities for hundreds of individuals to come together and have fun-filled, relaxing moments away from their little trailers (or some other less-than-optimal situations). For many, these particular evenings were the most joyful social times in their post-Katrina lives.

As time went on, we realized that repairing, restoring, or building a home was only the first step of recovery for the people of the Gulf Coast. Other forms of support were required for people to feel a sense of order. Community-oriented activities, support systems, caring for the caregivers, and developing compassionate leaders among the youth were some of the ways we tried to provide programs to move us towards a sense of normalcy. Our resiliency programs helped hundreds of caregivers in the hospitals, nursing homes, law enforcement agencies, teachers, and counselors in schools. We felt that if these individuals were empowered, they would be able to touch the lives of the people they served.

What a mighty God we serve! Little efforts initiated by us were becoming extra-ordinary moments of bonding, forming friendships, deepening relationships, and above all spreading the message of God's love. We did not have to preach about God's love and care, because everyone who walked in the door experienced the love and care of God firsthand.

CHAPTER 19

I Choose To Call These Miracles

Many touching stories come to my mind when I think of events that have happened since August 2005. The selfless acts of individuals and the organized efforts of the churches, faith-based groups, and others have been phenomenal. I have reached a point in my life that I do not accept that things happen accidentally or by chance. I believe there is a reason for everything that happens, even when I am not sure what that reason might be at the time.

The destruction Katrina caused was matched by the generosity of individuals. Hundreds of individuals contributed to the rebuilding efforts of St. Rose. What they donated varied, but the intent was one and the same—to offer a helping hand to those who were down. We may have received just ten dollars from a person or thousands from another. But we were touched and knew the generosity of their hearts spoke volumes of their desire to help us get back on our feet. Personally, receiving any donation from an individual or from an organization gave me a new perception of the real purpose for money. It is definitely not meant for hoarding. It cannot be taken with us when we leave this earth. Rather, it is meant to be used to make life comfortable for oneself or to make life a little more bearable for others. My heart was full with gratitude when I wrote a thank-you note to each of them.

Deborah Macon, the president of the Grantham University, Kansas City, Missouri (located in Slidell, Louisiana before the storm), sent a donation and wrote to me: "Many employees relocated with the university while others have remained in Slidell. It has been a difficult time, filled with mixed emotions for those in Kansas City as well as for those who are in Slidell and throughout the South. Yet we are grateful for the many blessings bestowed upon us by our Lord and Savior . . . Jermaine Labat sends greetings and is the reason for this contribution."

I received this beautiful note from Deacon Bill Heyman: "Greetings from St. John Vianney College seminary. As part of our continuing commitment to the people of the Gulf Coast region, the seminarians committed their Lenten contributions to St. Rose to assist in your ongoing recovery efforts" (these young men fasted and sent their food money to St. Rose).

Preston Smith from Dickinson College led a group of twenty young people to St. Rose. These young men and women worked and reiterated several times that it was a life changing experience for many of them. Looking at the enormity of our needs, Preston decided to put off his studies for another semester and took up a position with AmeriCorps to work on St. Rose's projects.

Another touching note from an elderly person: "I live on a fixed income. I do not have much to contribute. However, I will try to send in fifty dollars each month towards your tremendous efforts. May God give you strength."

I received a call from a couple from Colorado who wanted to respond to our Adopt-a-Child program. When I stated that it would take about thirty thousand dollars to provide half of the tuition assistance to all the children of St. Rose attending Catholic Schools, their response was "Consider it done." When they received our newsletters and found our recovery efforts credible, their support to our work in the community continued for another three years.

Can anyone call the following experience mere coincidence? Richard Gabe came to visit me in my office one afternoon. He had been coming to the Sunday Mass faithfully while volunteering at the Presbyterian Church in Bay St. Louis. He confided in me that his whole life had been transformed since Katrina. He had made a turnaround of his life since his arrival from the North. He was happy to work with the different groups that came to that church. For months he camped out at their parking lot and worked daily with the volunteers at the Presbyterian Church. On Ash Wednesday of 2006, he decided to go to a Catholic church, though he was not a practicing Catholic. He came to St. Rose for the first time but then kept coming back Sunday after Sunday. He also attended the three nights of Lenten revival preached by Deacon Art Miller from the Archdiocese of Hartford, Connecticut. These were purifying experiences for him, and he committed himself to the Lord once more.

After recounting these experiences he said, "I have been praying and toiling hard in my heart to make the right decision. My deceased mother's estate has been settled. I want to donate the money to the church with a clear conscience and with a sense of joy. I believe God has answered my prayers. I am here to donate the money, and it is thirteen thousand dollars."

I sat down stunned, but clearly touched by this man's journey. I cleared my throat and said, "I think you need to donate the money to the Presbyterian Church since that's where you've been volunteering for months. I am sure they will use the money for the people in need." He thanked me, we prayed and hugged each other, and he left my office. I felt a sense of joy in my heart for my words. Suddenly the selfish side in me spoke up, You are a fool to turn down that kind of money! I caught myself and once again thanked the Lord for the grace He gave me to respond the way I did to Mr. Gabe.

I continued to work in my office. It must have been less than twenty minutes later when another gentleman walked in my door. He introduced himself and said he had lived on Cedar Point in Bay St. Louis before the storm. He told me that his insurance claim was settled and that he wanted to donate to a church a portion of his claim. He told me that I would have the check for twenty thousand dollars the next day. I sat there again stunned! God works mysteriously.

The story didn't end there. Three days later Richard Gabe came back to me with a letter and a check for sixty-five hundred dollars. The letter read, "I have been on the beach praying about this. First I prayed to do it. Then I prayed that I would give this money freely. God answered my prayer this morning when I read Psalm 81. I can obey or disobey God; I could worship God or money. I give to St. Rose this check with joy in my heart. A matching check was given to the First Presbyterian Church."

On three occasions we considered ending our operation because of a lack of facilities to house volunteers. I believe that in some ways God intervened and made His purpose clear that we still had work to do. I thought about ending our operation by December 2006. We had to return the school back to Head Start. We did not know if we would have enough funds to continue the rebuilding efforts after the initial burst of donations and volunteers. To our amazement, churches, organizations, and individuals continued to support our efforts. When we had to move our volunteers out from the school buildings, families were willing to accommodate them in their homes. Then the idea of restoring the William J. Kelley, SVD Retreat Center surfaced.

While the volunteers worked on the retreat center, we were able to house them at The Gathering Place, owned by Bruce and Joanne Northridge (a former bed and breakfast facility they had cleaned up after five feet of floodwater came). Once the retreat center was completed, we were able to operate out of that facility for the next eighteen months. But the same questions surfaced when that eighteen-month term was coming to an end. At that point, the Mississippi Volunteer commission offered us twenty AmeriCorps positions. Where would we house them? God blessed us yet again. The United Jewish Foundation agreed to contribute one hundred thousand dollars, and the Vaz, Mirandy, and Dorsey families agreed to donate their vacant homes to house our volunteers in lieu of needed repairs on the homes.

More than five thousand volunteers! Working on more than five hundred homes! Offering services to thousands of individuals! Hundreds of thousands in monetary help! Hundreds of thousands of volunteer hours! For me, these are miracles. Several hurdles were present along the way, but God always made a way. There were clear signs of how God was able to open a window when a door was closed on us. As I indicated before, I do not believe in coincidences. I believe that everything happens for a reason, even when I do not know what that reason is. I am not able to come up with an answer to the question, "Why couldn't God have prevented Katrina from happening?" However, I have come up with these two conclusions in my heart: that even in the midst of great trials and struggles, (1) so much good has been shown, and (2) ultimately God has the final say. I have experienced the awesome presence, protection, and guidance of God through it all. I have seen how God can take the little we have and multiply it into abundance.

Look at the story of Eight Days of Hope, an organization St. Rose worked closely with:

> Eight Days of Hope was meant to be a one-time visit to the Gulf Coast with a handful of people after Hurricane Katrina. God allowed this ministry to blossom into so much more! On six different occasions, thousands of volunteers have ministered to people's needs and have helped them put their lives back in order after Hurricane Katrina, Hurricane Rita, and the floods in Cedar Rapids, Iowa. Eight Days of Hope has one goal! Love people and serve people as Jesus loves us!

- 6,448 volunteers have participated in these relief efforts!
- Eight Days of Hope has remodeled, refurbished or rebuilt 954 homes!
- 15,600 pieces of Sheetrock have been installed!
- 3,200 squares of roofing shingles have been nailed on roofs!
- 305 homes have completely or partially been rewired!
- Over 2,300 rolls of insulation have been installed!
- 63 homes have been primed and painted!
- 405 homes have had extensive carpentry work done!

More than 9.3 million dollars worth of labor have been donated through Eight Days of Hope!

Volunteers from forty-three states and multiple countries have shown up to work! In fact over 186,000 man-hours have been worked during these six trips! The real story behind Eight Days of Hope is the impact on the lives of homeowners and volunteers that are being changed forever through these relief efforts. On these six trips, our volunteers have come to bless others only to go home feeling like they were the ones being blessed.

In the first book of Peter 4:10, he tells us to use the gifts that God has given us to minister to one another. Eight Days of Hope plans to live this call out during our mission trips to areas affected by natural disasters.

Please continue learning more about this grassroots effort wanting and willing to sacrifice in order to bring hope to those in need. The number eight means, "new beginnings."

Our prayer is that you will feel called to make a difference with us one home and more importantly one life at a time. Help bring a new beginning to families who are feeling hopeless.

May God bless you as you consider how you can make a difference with Eight Days of Hope!

Stephen Tybor III, President, Eight Days of Hope
(Taken from the Eight Days of Hope website)

The tiny seed of inspiration produced abundant fruits. I love the scene in the gospel where the miraculous multiplication of the loaves is described. In the gospel of Matthew, this narrative is immediately after the beheading of John the Baptist, the herald of the Messiah. After hearing about the merciless murder of His cousin, Jesus withdrew to a deserted place, probably wanting to be alone. The entire text is very powerful:

When Jesus heard of it, He withdrew in a boat to a deserted place by Himself. The crowds heard of this and followed Him on foot from their towns. When He disembarked and saw the vast crowd, His heart was moved with pity for them, and He cured their sick. When it was evening, the disciples approached Him and said, "This is a deserted place and it is already late;

dismiss the crowds so that they can go into the villages and buy food for themselves." Jesus said to them, "There is no need for them to go away; give them some food yourselves." But they said to Him, "Five loaves and two fish are all we have here.' Then He said "Bring them here to me," and He ordered the crowds to sit down on the grass. Taking the five loaves and two fish, and looking up to heaven, He said the blessing, broke the loaves, and gave them to His disciples, who in turn gave them to the crowds. They all ate and were satisfied, and they picked up the fragments left over—twelve wicker baskets full. Those who ate were about five thousand men, not counting women and chil-dren (Matthew 14:13-21).

I can draw a few parallels between this scene and our experi-ence of Katrina. In many ways we were like the disciples who found the situation very hard to handle. They only had five loaves and two fishes. The needs were too many, and the re-sources were too little. The words and actions of Jesus are very powerful. First of all, He ordered them to sit down. For me it is a beautiful way of dealing with hardships in life—sit down in the presence of God. This sitting down helps us think clearly and prepares us to receive what God has in store for us. Some of us don't like to be recipients but only givers. But the truth is that, in some form, all of us are recipients; and after Katrina, all of us received something in some form.

Secondly, He asked them to bring the little they had to Him. Their little resource soon was multiplied in the hands of Jesus. I believe that when we bring before God the little we have with a trusting spirit, He can multiply it beyond our imagina-tion. In our lives we saw people bringing their little and these becoming abundant in the process.

Thirdly, their need was met and they were satisfied. In some form, our needs were met, and we felt a sense of satisfaction. I am not naïve to claim that every need of every person was met. If we are honest with ourselves, we can say, "Yes, I feel satisfied."

Finally, Jesus asked them to collect the leftovers. From our experiences, it is important that we collect the lessons of life for tomorrow. These "leftovers" can be powerful tools for dealing with the struggles that come into our lives.

There are two ways to live your life. One is as though nothing is a miracle. The other is as though everything is a miracle (Albert Einstein).

CONCLUSION

Katrina will always be remembered for the pain and suffering that it brought to the residents of the Gulf Coast. The powerful wind blew things apart; the monstrous storm surge scattered things all around. Yet nothing could stop us from coming together. Ultimately we were not blown apart, but *Blown Together*. In many ways it brought out the best in us. The strength of character that was exhibited, the power of faith that was lived out, the hope that was kept alive, and the outpouring of compassion and generosity that we received are all indications of so much good that is present in this world. Tragedies and crises have a way of bringing people together. We all have benefited so much from Katrina's trials. Though there are many things that we want to forget, the lessons and miracles from all of this are to be remembered forever.

True, Katrina was an anomaly, hopefully a onetime occurrence. Yet, personal "Katrinas" take place in our daily lives. If we have learned the lessons of life from this monstrous storm, we will have with us some tools to deal with the Katrinas of our lives. The lessons of love, compassion, kindness, care, service, faith, prayers, and sharing that came about because of this storm called Katrina will help us to deal with the storms of life. We will have the conviction in our hearts that God, who strengthened us in days past, will continue to give us His grace and strength. The realization that "Katrina was big, but God is bigger" will foster a renewed spirit within us to deal with the trials of life. The conviction that we are never alone, but are accompanied by the grace of God and the support of people of goodwill, can sustain us in moments of crisis. Ultimately, all of this can lead us to a firm belief that we are all, in so many ways, called to be our brother's and sister's keeper.

The light shines in the darkness and the darkness could not overcome it (John 1:5).

TESTIMONIES

The following are testimonies from some of the people who were touched by Katrina, who saw the miracles that God orchestrated, and who contributed to them.

Forever I Will Cling to My God
Florence Jordan

I give all honor and glory to you my Lord! My name is Florence Jordan. I am married to my childhood sweetheart, Paul, for thirty-eight years. God has blessed us with three children: Paul Jr., Monroe, and daughter Alicia. Alicia is no longer with us because God took her home ten years ago. I have worked in the school system for twenty-two years, and I love working with children very much. My heart has so much joy working with children.

I wanted to tell you about Alicia because she is a very important part of this story. Alicia died almost six years before Katrina rolled into Waveland, Mississippi. It was so hard to go in her room to pack up her things after she died. I would try but I just couldn't, so I decided to just leave the room the way she left it. Since I had not been able to remove her things for so long, I just felt like God knew that it was time, so He came in with a mighty storm and did it for me. It still was hard on us to put her things out on the side of the road afterwards; it was like losing her all over again. But God was right there in the midst of it all, giving Paul the strength to do what had to be done. People used to ask me how I felt about losing my home. I told them the only thing I hated losing were the pictures of my children and some of their baby things. Those were things that meant so much to me ... things that I just could not replace. The rest was just stuff.

Yes, Katrina came and took things away from us and changed our lives; but it also gave my family and others something better. We were given the gift of faith that there are still a lot of good people in this world, and God's love continues to shine!

When I was seventeen years old, Hurricane Camille came through the town of Clermont Harbor, Mississippi, and I had to get on top of our house because Daddy hadn't thought that anything would happen. Well it was at night and I was extremely frightened, so I told my boyfriend (Paul) that I would never again stay for a hurricane. After we were married we would evacuate whenever there was news about a hurricane coming our way. Our family and friends would laugh at us because nothing major ever happened during those times. We would travel through bad weather and traffic. When the storm had passed, we would call back to Waveland, and they would tell us things were fine. This happened for years.

This time when we heard that a hurricane was coming, I started getting clothes packed so we could leave. Paul and I watched the news, waiting and hoping that it would not hit here. When we finally realized that we had to leave, I called my family in New Orleans and started making plans about when we were going to leave and where we were going. They told us that they would make reservations in Houston, Texas. When I told Paul that we had to get out of here, he said okay, but we would go to church first, and then we would leave.

We went to church and informed the few friends who were in attendance and Father Sebastian that we were evacuating. He jokingly said, "Don't be a chicken." Paul decided to stay. Sometimes I feel that I stayed because I didn't want to be called "chicken"!

Anyway, the weather started getting bad, and the water

started coming in the house. I told my grandson Tre to run and get in the attic. When we got up to the attic, I looked down and the water was rising faster. Paul was still downstairs getting food and our medicine. Thank God that he picked up my purse (it had my phone in it). I sat on the edge of the attic stairs, but the rising water covered the steps. When the attic door closed, I told Paul we were going to die. He said, "Baby, we are not going to die." He held up a knife and said, "I will cut a hole in the attic so we can get out if we have to."

I started praying and talking to God, letting Him know that I remembered the promise He made many years ago about not destroying this land by water. I told Him if He had to take someone to please take me and not my grandson. I took my grandson in my arms. I stretched out my hand and told God, "You have got to stop this water right now." Paul was praying and cutting a hole in the attic so that we could get on top of the roof. God is so good for suddenly the water stopped rising. We stayed up there for hours. While we were just sitting there in the attic, I asked Paul to look me in my eyes and I said, "Promise me you will never do this again." He said, "Baby, I promise."

I was so afraid. I didn't know if our son Paul Jr. was all right. I was praying and asking God to please take care of him. I just wanted Him to let me know that my son was all right. When we finally came out of the attic and went out to the street we saw him. The roof of his house had blown away except for one spot … and that is where he had stayed during the entire ordeal. We began to check out the level of destruction, and it was overwhelming. We found out that our neighbor's husband was missing and that his mother had died. We were glad to be alive and yet sad to hear about the deaths of people in the community.

When I first came out of the attic, I could see my house was destroyed; mud was everywhere; our furniture was all over the place. I looked at everything, and I asked God for only one thing. When my daughter died, my husband had a pendant made for me with a picture of Alicia. I told God all I wanted was that pendant. God is so good; He will give you the desires of your heart. I went in our room that was now full of mess. I knew where the dresser had been, so I figured it had to have fallen there. I put my hand in that mess and felt all around, and all I saw was the back of the pendant. I picked it up, turned it over, and wiped off the mud, and it was in good shape. I thanked Jesus and walked out of that house.

After coming out of the attic and seeing the devastation, we didn't know what to do. We sat under our carport all day just looking and wondering what to do next. Neighbors started coming out of their homes. My wonderful husband (who I consider a superman because he can do anything) was thinking as usual. He told some of the men that they could get chain saws going to cut the trees out of the way so we could walk to the highway. They worked on four wheelers. We started gathering old women and children in car trailers and pulling them out by hand to Highway 90. We sat there all day waiting for someone to come. A truck came and took the people to Bay High School. People started getting four wheelers working and were using them for transportation. Paul and some other people decided to continue to work while waiting for any of the disaster agencies to arrive.

Three days later I had another miracle. My father-in-law came back to Waveland to check on us. I asked him to take me to the Bay Bridge because I heard that we could get a signal there to use our cell phones. I tried calling my family to let them know that we were all right. I was not able to get anyone. While I was still trying, my phone started to ring. When I answered, it was my cousin from Dallas. He said, "My God, we thought you were all dead." I always said that was a miracle for me to be at the bridge at that time when the call came through.

A church from West Point, Louisiana, sent a van to pick up people. I stayed because I didn't want to leave Paul. Later he convinced me to leave with my cousins as it was better for our grandson Tre to be out of the devastation. I agreed and waited for the arrival of my cousins from Dallas.

The police and volunteers started coming and bringing water and food. We set up camp on a street that didn't have a lot of mud. We cooked and tried to keep ourselves safe.

Three days later my cousins showed up with vans to take us to Dallas where I stayed until October. The school district called and informed us that FEMA was sending house trailers so we could get the schools started again. They put us on a list. I just kept thinking what I could do to get closer to home. Then I thought about my brother-in-law who buys houses and fixes them up to rent. I called my sister and asked if Carl had anything. She said she would have him call when he got home. Later on that night he called and said a lady was just leaving, and I could come and stay in the house. He said he had to clean it up and fix some things. I told my family in Dallas that I was sorry, but I was going to Covington, Louisiana, which was much closer to home. I had one of my cousins from Houston come and get me and drive me to Covington. I called Paul and told him that I was coming home. All I could think about was getting closer to my home and my church. I really missed being at St. Rose, worshiping with the community, and singing with the choir. When I heard that they had services, I ached because I was not there.

Paul's cousin fixed up a truck so we could have something to ride in. It wasn't the best truck, but Paul was able to come to

Covington and pick me up for church. Then our trailer came in October. I was able to leave Covington and return to Waveland. It was a very happy moment. When I look back, I realize it didn't take much for us to be happy in those days.

I wanted to give back something to people just like people gave to us while we were in Covington. St. Rose had formed the Hurricane Task Force under the leadership of Father Sebastian. There were people coming in to help with cooking, building houses, repairing homes, and giving people clothes and household goods. St Rose was basically trying to do anything the people needed to get their lives back. There were a lot of things going on, and I wanted to be part of giving and not merely taking.

People came from all over world to help us. It was such a wonderful experience. I always said there were good and bad things that came from Katrina. I am so thankful that God saw fit to spare my family members. I have had a lot of things happen to me in my life, but I never stopped believing that God would see me through it all. And I am still holding on to God's hands. I just want to praise and worship Him until I leave this earth and see my daughter Alicia and my mother and father again.

I am so grateful for Father Sebastian. Paul and I believe that God sent him because he knew that we would need a strong leader. He was that and so much more. When Paul and I were grieving the loss of our daughter, he helped us get through that difficult time. Then Katrina came and he was there to help again. Paul and I are so grateful for all that he has done for us. He also helped my son (Paul Jr.) find his way back to Jesus. Words cannot express how we feel about this wonderful man of God.

There is a song I used to sing when I was a little girl. It says

"Without God, I could do nothing. Without him, I would fail. Without God, my life would be so rugged, like a ship without a sail. That is why I will forever cling to my God."

Florence Collins Jordan was born in New Orleans and moved to Waveland, MS. She has been married to Paul Jordan, Sr. for thirty-nine years and been blessed with three children. She has been employed in the Bay-Waveland School system for the last twenty-two years. She is a very committed member of St. Rose Church and St. Rose Gospel choir.

Miracles, Miracles, and More Miracles!

Marilyn Smith

My brothers, sister, and I had a healthy life growing up in Bay St. Louis. That was a miracle. We had food, clothes, a church, and a Catholic school to attend. We had our faith, and what a blessing that was! That's where my devotion began. I thank God today for that experience of growing up as a child in the town of Bay St. Louis, with a church and school that I loved so dearly. St. Rose de Lima was the center of my joy! Where else could you get an education with master teachers from first grade to twelfth grade for $4.25 a month and lunch for $1.00 a week? I cherish this place and that is one of my miracles. To be baptized, make first Holy Communion, be confirmed as an adult in the church, take marriage vows, confess, and still be hanging in here—that is a miracle! My miracles are many at St. Rose, and they continue to happen on a daily basis.

So many wonderful religious and clergy have come through the doors of St. Rose, bringing the love of Jesus, spreading the word of God, and helping us to understand that we are all children of God. What other place but St. Rose de Lima in Bay St. Louis could have instilled such an impression on a young girl named Marilyn Elizabeth Smith? I can't say enough about my growing up experiences and my life in this town. After graduation, I entered the convent of the Sisters of the Holy Family in New Orleans. In my first year at Holy Family as a postulant, I completed my first year of college at Delille Jr. College. After that year, in 1966, I decided to enter Dillard University, a couple blocks down the highway, where I received a Bachelor of Arts degree in Education. After working and teaching in New Orleans for a couple of years, I returned to Bay St. Louis to begin my ministry at St. Rose de Lima, my favorite place to be. In the meantime I had come to the realization that God was

110

calling me to another form of life that involved the roles of a wife, mother, and teacher. I knew with all these I could still serve Him and His people.

In 1969, I had the opportunity to purchase an old home, which was built in 1948 (the year that I was born) from one of my relatives. Muriel was actually my grandfather's niece. I lived there for years, even through Hurricane Camille. I took shelter at my mom and dad's brick home rather than stay in my wooden frame house, although it survived Camille, and I was able to return home. Our family was intact; our homes were intact; our possessions were still ours. The community was on the rise again. We had a number of years to recoup from Camille. Katrina swept through Bay St. Louis thirty-five years later, and there we were again, looking for a miracle to restore us to new life and health.

When Katrina struck we were all at the old homestead, the home that my dad built for us. This is where we would all come together because this house my dad, Ed, built was considered "the house that Jack built" (especially after the Aretha Franklin song came out). It was sturdy and well built, with cinder blocks and cement poured between the walls. We had survived many other storms in this location.

On the fourth day after Katrina struck, it became apparent we could no longer stay in these conditions. My daughter Emleigh and son-in-law Lemond drove through barricades and roadblocks to get us and take us back to Houston, Texas. We stayed in Houston for six weeks and then returned to Bay St. Louis for the grandsons to return to school, for their mother to return to work, and for me to begin my ministry with St. Rose. When I returned, the entire school building had become a center for the community to come for relief. There were clothes from floor to ceiling. Truckloads of goods and items were being delivered from all over the country for the relief of the people who needed the smallest items from a toothbrush to tables and chairs and beds and bed linens that were so needed during this time.

It was heartwarming to serve the people of the area, to be able to supply them with the staples that they needed in the process of recovery. St. Rose de Lima Catholic elementary and high school had become the General Store, the Days Inn, and a place also to restore ourselves to spiritual health. Our pastor, Father Sebastian, was the ringleader and the glue that kept it all together. The outpouring and the love that came through this church to the town was a remarkable miracle. Our people were restored to new health, to a livelihood that we once took for granted, to the realization that our faith in God is what brought us through this stormy period in our lives. Thank you, God. Thank you, Father Sebastian. Thank you to the people who flocked here to make this place better than it was.

We survived Katrina! We were truly blessed. Some were not as fortunate as others but miracle of all miracles, we had people from all over this country swooping down on this little town of Bay St. Louis to help us restore ourselves to a new and better life. The first two respondents that really brought a difference to my life were a young married couple from New York. Brian and Loretta Treffeisen were sent by God himself to work miracles in our town. Loretta cooked and cleaned and worked and set up schedules for workers and did all that it took to make residents and workers comfortable. Brian—we can call him a Master Builder—soon began working on projects that St. Rose had initiated. You see God makes people in His own image—Jesus, the Son of God, was a carpenter, a Master Builder so to speak. Brian, a man after God's own heart, ended up being the contractor for the rebuilding of my home, which was totally destroyed by Katrina. Another young man named Beau Saccoccia was also a motivating factor for me in the rebuilding of my home.

I had no idea how I would be able to rebuild my house. Beau said that I should fill out the paperwork, and we'd figure something out. The paperwork got filled out, the foundation and the house went up, and Marilyn was a new homeowner. Those who were instrumental in building my home were of course my pastor, Father Sebastian Myladiyil, SVD; the young AmeriCorps volunteers; people from all across this country; and our adopted church family from Holy Trinity Catholic church in Washington, D.C. How do you give back to so many who have done so much for you? Where do you start? Well, if you knew how to cook, that was a start because all of our responders had to eat, and they had to have somewhere to sleep. We at St. Rose were able to provide places for our extended families to sleep and eat. Those of us who had trailers were able to share spaces for the waves of people who came through from Washington, D.C. to the state of Washington. It was a joy to house Margie Legowski from Holy Trinity, and Molly Evans and her family and friends from Seattle, Washington.

Did I face trials among miracles or miracles among trials? I consider my life to be a series of miracles. There are trials that are part of my life. However, I see God's unseen hand working miraculously through them all for my betterment. On my own, I knew I would not be able to rebuild my home. Who would have thought that an aged old home that had been in the family for sixty plus years would now be replaced by a new one, built by friends from all over this country and India? Miracles happen on a daily basis in this little town of Bay St. Louis. So many people have crossed my path in friendship and love. I have my church family to thank for their support in my recovery efforts.

Our friends from Washington, D.C. thought enough of us to put our parishioners on a bus to DC and give us the grand tour of our nation's Capitol. The effort was to take us out of the stress and worry of our situation in Bay St. Louis. What wonderful friendships were borne out of a tragedy called Katrina! The people of Holy Trinity Parish are still part of our family of St. Rose today. I know of one little miracle that came about because of our close relationship—our little Catholic school, once Bay Catholic Elementary School, now bears the name of Holy Trinity Elementary. That was a blessing for us and our children.

I feel privileged and honored to have met and worked with John & Ann Hisle and Margie Legowski from DC, Mary Coyne from Diamondhead, Mississippi, and Lin & Jerald Jackson from Hattiesburg, Mississippi. The connections never cease; that is a miracle and that is the best part of allowing another person to be part of your life and making friends.

Our story is out there. In fact, we at St. Rose have been the focus of a number of short videos that have been made a part of the Archives of History for the State of Mississippi! Our story now includes the many who have come to our aid … many who have become lifelong friends. What a miracle to behold!

My pastor says "If you see a good person, imitate him or her; if you see a bad person, examine your conscience." All the volunteers who have made their way to beautiful, wonderful Bay St. Louis should be imitated, admired, and thanked to the highest heavens. What miracles to behold! When I see you, I see Jesus. What would Jesus do? He would do the same things that our friends from near and far did for us when we were down and out. Are you looking for a miracle? Look at me!

Marilyn Smith is a retired educator from the Harrison County School system. After teaching for 31 years she has committed her life fully to the ministries of the church. She is currently employed by the SVDs to manage the William J. Kelley, SVD Retreat Center in Bay St. Louis, MS.

"The Way We Were"

Kathe Calhoun

I am Kathe Calhoun, an older senior citizen, not aging too gracefully, living on a fixed income and the sales of my artwork.

There are many times in our lives that seem almost impossible to overcome ... then came Katrina—the worst natural cataclysm in the history of the United States (cataclysm: a great flood, deluge, any great upheaval, as in earthquake or a war, that causes sudden and violent changes). A real awakening!

Unable to evacuate due to major surgery (a total knee replacement) just days before the storm, I awakened the next morning to the miracle that I was still alive due to the help of friends (John Harris and Ed Jurkowski) who insisted I come to their home to weather the storm. First there were seven of us who had watched the storm on a wind-up TV and prayed. I was given the job of making sure the candle in front of the statue of the Virgin Mary never went out. That wasn't too hard to do since candlelight was our only light. When it was all over and the boards taken down from the windows, we saw for the first time the total devastation before us. It wasn't long before people started walking, crying, and just staring, unable to fathom that they no longer had a place to live, much less food, water, clothes, or cars. The seven of us soon became many more. Before too long our supplies of water were almost depleted. Some good thinking and the finding of a large white sheet and a can of black spray proved to be very useful. "We need water" was spray painted on the sheet and put out on an open space between the fallen trees, and in a short time trucks from the National Guard rolled in with the much needed water. What a blessing! Very quickly you become aware of the forces of Mother Nature.

I found out that I was one of the lucky ones. I still had a

home even though it was a flooded wreck. I felt lucky to still have a few pieces of clothing, some keepsakes, and most of all many of my friends. (Some of them eventually had to leave due to fear, cost of rebuilding, insurance and numerous other reasons, and I consider that to be another great loss.)

Help came from so many. On the Friday after the storm, my son Haven was able to get an angel flight into Gulfport and got the only rental car with gas. He arrived in Bay St. Louis, and picked me up to take me to his home in Marietta, Georgia. Unfortunately when we finally got back to the airport, we were informed the airport was under lockdown, and the plane had been directed to leave. Never have I sat in an airport alone (except for being with my son who was talking and doing everything he could to get a plane to come back, with FAA approval, to pick us up but to no avail). As the hours went by, my only company was numerous soldiers with machine guns. They didn't come too close as I hadn't had a bath in five days and wore dirty clothes and a leg bandage that looked like I had crawled through the trenches. I guess they figured I wasn't too much of a threat, and I'm sure they didn't want to get too near.

After several hours of this, we decided to just take the car and drive as far as we could on the gas we had left. That was a real scary ordeal. After sitting in line at a gas station somewhere in either Alabama or Georgia for nearly an hour, we were informed that they had run out of gas about five cars ahead of us. All of us were turned away but once again my son did some pleading and asked the owner of the station to tell us where the next possible place was to obtain some gas. We were able to get there, filled up, and started on our way again. We drove through dark cities and around so many detours. We saw people sleeping on top of bridges or anywhere that was mostly safe and dry. Trying to stop at a motel was no better. No electricity meant

116

that the people who were already there were all standing on the balconies with their room doors open, trying to get some air on a stifling early September night.

We finally arrived in Marietta and after a tearful reunion I headed for a wonderful shower and sleep. I was clean, safe, and with family; and because of this, I was allowed to heal both physically and emotionally. Thanks to Starlet, my daughter-in-law, who on more than one occasion stood in long lines and helped when I just about lost it after an insurance company told me they had no record of my filing anything with them after I had been on the phone with them day after day! When she saw my frustration, she took the phone from me and stayed on it until she got results.

The loss of my car was mind-blowing with no replacement for seven and a half months. The insurance company was not to blame, but the bank that had carried the financing in Georgia had messed up and said there was a lien on the car (it had been paid off two years before). It took forever to clear up the situation since I no longer had any paperwork to prove it. Phone calls were nearly impossible, and sending and receiving mail was even worse. It also meant that I had to ask friends to get me to the post office every few days. These dear people gave up their efforts at recovery and used what little costly gasoline they had to help me. When I finally received a clear title to the car it wasn't my car—not even the same make or color. Nothing was correct about the document; only my name was right. On top of this, my mail was going into orbit somewhere, and Fr. Sebastian suggested that I give them the church address. It took sending a total of three copies before the correct one was received at the church. I was really beginning to wonder as to how many mistakes could be made on one document. Now as I look back at the number of hours it took, I think that maybe this "busy" time just helped the days go faster and made me not think so much of the smell and filth that still lingered outside my trailer.

At first the loss of 95 percent of my studio, supplies, and a collection of nearly thirty-five years of reference work, paintings, prints, and all the inventory seemed impossible to overcome. Then the Arts of Hancock stepped in and arranged for numerous art shows across America. I was able to attend three of these shows, but found it too difficult after not having therapy on my knee for eight and a half months. More help came; the Mississippi Arts Commission awarded me a grant that allowed me to replace what was needed in my studio to continue my artwork.

Sometime before this, a friend had given me a few supplies, and I found myself sitting in my trailer and listening to a donated radio when the song "The Way We Were" began playing. With tears in my eyes I couldn't help but think how appropriate that song was. The words "misty watercolor memories" made me pick up the few supplies I had, and I did my first painting since Katrina. I called it *The Way We Were*, and I donated that watercolor painting to St. Rose. It became a very successful fundraiser for the church. Sometimes inspiration comes to us in the most unusual ways. Or was this God's way to strengthen me to face all the hardships and unknowns of rebuilding? After all, I still had a home even though it had to be gutted and rebuilt. How lucky I was—so many had nothing left! At this point I realized I had to let God take the lead in my life. He ended up playing such a big part in rebuilding my home ... and in rebuilding me. And He is still working on me!

FEMA trailers—there were many times we all complained about the problems with them ... but do you know of any other country in the world that would furnish you a place to live while rebuilding?

Many of the volunteers found a new purpose in their lives by helping those who had lost so much. I am still receiving letters, phone calls, emails and visits from many of them. How wonderful of them. God does work in mysterious ways.

Will I ever be able to thank all the wonderful volunteers, and St. Rose de Lima, and First Baptist Church-Main St., who gave so freely of their precious time, money, and encouragement? Probably not, but they all will remain in my daily prayers.

Kathe Calhoun moved to Bay St. Louis in 1994. Kathe's parents maintained a place in Bay St. Louis and she came to the Bay often as a child and in later years with her own children. She is a professional artist and has produced numerous pieces of art that are loved by people across the country.

I Still Love the Water

LiLi Stahler

My husband, George, and I had moved to Waveland in 2001. We had started a business in Metairie in 1980, ran it for twenty years, then sold it and retired. My parents had a weekend cottage, the Green House, in Waveland, Mississippi; and I had grown up spending weekends and summers there. Our children had grown up with Waveland as a second home. George added on to the cottage and in August 2001, it became our home.

We loved living on the Coast and being near the water. It was a glorious retirement. We were active members of St. Rose de Lima Catholic Church and enjoyed the warm vibrant church community. St. Rose was the source for our spiritual life as well as social life. I did publicity and public relations for the parish, and George was one of the founding members of the Men's Gospel Ensemble. George had slowed down a bit after having been diagnosed with Chronic Obstructive Pulmonary Disease (COPD). Still, we enjoyed our life in Waveland and on the Coast.

Several days before Hurricane Katrina hit, as it loomed up before us, we made the decision to ride it out at home. We live on the north side of the tracks, and our Green House had stood through hurricanes for over a hundred years. Our godchild, Liz Ferguson, lived in Waveland south of the tracks. She did not want to evacuate, and we told her that she could come stay with us as we would be safe in the Green House. I even assured her mother, a lifelong friend, that all would be well with us. When Katrina hit, Liz and her dog Little were in a small raised guest house, the Red House, on our property.

I have no conception of time during the storm. We lost power early. We had communication with Liz by walkie-talkies.

Our property had quite a lot of trees, and we watched them fall. A large oak fell through the back of our house, taking the roof, attic, and a bathroom with it. We put a large screw in the door to hold it to the door frame, but the heavy rains came into the house. George and I were standing in the middle of the den when we felt the floor rise beneath us. We looked out onto the porch and saw that water had flooded the porch and was about a foot above the doorsill. It wasn't rainwater. Water from the Mississippi Sound had come as far as our house. We had to open a door to equalize the pressure as we were literally floating off our foundation. When the water rushed in, it leveled off at about two feet. As our house is three and a half feet off the ground, we had about five and a half feet of water on the property. The water receded as quickly as it came in, leaving dark, sticky, oily mud on the floors and furniture. Everything from two feet down was ruined. I don't think we ever mourned the loss of our trees and possessions. So many lives were lost and so many families had lost so much more. Liz had lost her home and everything in it. We started on the process of surviving—looking for water, food, and shelter.

It was the following morning when we began to realize the total devastation that Waveland and the Coast had suffered. Liz and I walked the mile to Highway 90, climbing over trees in the road and through debris, and headed for the Waveland Police Department. Surely they would have some communication with the outside world and could contact our families. We didn't realize at the time that more water had flooded the highway north of us than we had experienced at our house. The police had ridden out the storm clinging to tree branches at the police station that had been under water. There was no communication—cell phones didn't work. Our families were scattered throughout several states, and we had no way of letting them know that we were alive until days later when we finally made contact with them. We were joyful and at the same time felt devastated because we were causing them such worry and that there was nothing we could do about it. Walking down the highway we saw our fellow church members, Florence and Paul Jordan. They told us that people had died in their neighborhood. We were beginning to realize more and more how devastating this storm had been to all of us and to our community.

Again, I have no concept of days. Shortly after the storm, Bruce Northridge (another church member) came by on a bike and informed us that St. Rose had survived with little damage. Our pastor, Fr. Sebastian, also came by to see how we were. One could see people outside cooking whatever was in their freezer, because as things defrosted, there was no way to keep them cool.

Our son-in-law arranged for us to get a John Deere Gator delivered from Houma, Louisiana. George's truck, my car, and Liz's car had all been underwater and were inoperable. We used the Gator to go to the highway where stations were set up for ice, food, and water. This was a daily trip. The first Sunday after the storm, I don't remember how we got word that the bishop would be celebrating Mass at St. Rose. I do remember that we went in the Gator. There was no light in the church, the carpet was wet, and everyone was crying. The tears were that of joy to be alive, thanksgiving that we had survived and our beloved church building was still standing, and tears of grief for those who had perished and for those who had lost everything.

I didn't realize then what a miracle it was that St. Rose was spared. There was a reason! St. Rose led the area in recovery and rebuilding. We learned over the next months and years what great joy and compassion can come out of a disaster. Volunteers from all over the world found their way to St. Rose. Lodging was prepared for those who came to our aid. Food, household items, and clothing came by the truckload. And although St. Rose had always been a loving community, our bonds with each other became stronger. Neighbors helped neighbors. All of us were in this together.

When we had replaced the floors and Sheetrock in our house, we were able to open it to volunteers. That was March of '06. Our first volunteers were twins, Molly and Jen Feltner. Jen lived in D.C. and had volunteered as her church, Holy Trinity, had partnered with St. Rose in the recovery effort. She enlisted her sister and they came for a week. They learned roofing and came to love our area. (They have been back to visit several times.) Jen quit her job in D.C. and came to volunteer for a year. The next volunteers we housed were roofers from Hastings, Michigan. They did an awesome job in getting roofs back on houses.

Waveland—referred to as "Ground Zero"—lost all public buildings. From tents and trailers, the city ran all government functions, including the Fire and Police Departments. It was a challenging time, and it was a year after Katrina when I decided to run for public office. When I asked Fr. Sebastian what he thought about my running, he said that working for my community was a ministry just as much as working for St. Rose. I put all my energy into campaigning and won a spot on the Board. When I think back about the challenges facing our community and my lack of experience, I wonder how and why I ever thought I could help. But those were challenging times, and all of us found strength we didn't know we had. We didn't have time to worry or wonder if we were doing things correctly.

There was so much to do, so we just started doing what we could. I really didn't think about it at the time; but now reflecting on what we did and are still doing, I realize that it was the hand of God that guided us. We found inner strength through our church, our community, and our neighbors. We became more compassionate. We were actually better people and had grown spiritually through this experience. For each one of us, it was a small miracle. For our entire Coast it was a huge miracle. God moves in ways unbeknownst to us. I often say that I wouldn't recommend a disaster to anyone, but it certainly made us better people.

I have learned what it really means to give thanks, and I've also learned what is important and what is not. The glory of God and His mercy were shown every day. Through our church community, we were blessed with literally thousands of volunteers. Each one tried to help in his or her unique way. Each one made a mark. Besides helping with rebuilding homes, they helped rebuild lives. Amazingly, the volunteers thanked us. They said that we gave to them much more than they gave to us. I still haven't figured that out yet. Maybe our strength encouraged them to be strong.

On April 10, 2010, the city of Waveland cut the ribbon on our new pier. The Garfield Ladner Memorial Pier had been built, rebuilt after Hurricane Camille, and now rebuilt once more. Four years and seven months after Hurricane Katrina, we can, once again, walk out on the pier. Children and adults alike can fish or just sit.

It's out on the water that I feel closest to God. I've walked to the end of the pier and watched the sun rise the last two mornings. The sunrise is beautiful; the weather is beautiful. One day the water was calm; one day there were waves. I love being out on the water. Although that same water destroyed a way of life, I have found another way. I'm not afraid, for God is with me.

Lili Stahler moved to Waveland in 2001. Ever since her childhood she spent her summers in Waveland, MS. She is an active member of St. Rose community and an elected official for the City of Waveland. She is very outspoken and known for her passion and enthusiasm.

"Katrina Was Big, But God Is Bigger"

(Sign in Front of St. Clare Church
Two Weeks After the Storm)

Noel Phillips

My name is Noel Phillips, and I live in Waveland, Mississippi, with my wife, Betsy. At the time of the storm, my brother Bill, my son Peter, and our dog Izzy lived with us. Betsy and I have been residents of Waveland for over thirty years, and we are members of St. Clare Parish. I have served in many capacities and ministries at St. Clare over the years, and I have served as Director of St. Clare Recovery for the last five years. Before I retired and before Katrina, I was the owner of Dolphin Press Inc., a printing company in Long Beach, Mississippi.

We knew a large storm called Katrina was forming in the Gulf of Mexico, but living on the Mississippi Gulf Coast and in New Orleans all our lives, we had weathered many storms and hurricanes. What was the big deal about this storm? We had survived Camille when we lived north of the railroad tracks (which served as a levee for that part of Waveland). My family and neighbors made the decision that we would stay and weather the storm. But little did we know that this was "THE BIG ONE."

On the morning of the storm, Betsy, Peter, Bill, and I were looking out the front door watching a pine tree fall on our car when we noticed the water coming up our front steps. When it reached our knees, we went out the back door and waded through water up to our necks to Cherri and Bill McIntyre's (my sister and brother-in-law) house next door as their house was higher than ours and had two stories. Luckily the water barely got into Cherri's house and then receded. We stood on their porch and watched our furniture floating inside our house. Can you imagine a twenty-five inch console TV floating?

At that time, we did not know that Waveland was destroyed along with St. Clare church, rectory, convent, parish hall, and school. All that was left of the convent and rectory were concrete slabs. In fact, every structure on the south side of the railroad tracks no longer existed.

The day after the storm, Waveland's Chief of Police Jimmy Varnell, Fr. Gillespie from St. Clare's, Fr. Gillespie's brother, and I made it to Coleman Avenue (the business district of Waveland). We climbed to the top of an eight-foot pile of debris, and we gasped. When we saw nothing left standing from where we were all the way to the beach, we all cried.

Since there were no communications in or out of the area—no cell phones or land lines—our families and friends did not know if we were alive or dead. It had been announced on national TV that Waveland was destroyed. Our daughter Lulie had been living in Gulfport during Katrina and thought we were all dead. Nobody was allowed into Waveland except the National Guard, but somehow she managed to get through and arrived at my sister's house on Wednesday to find us alive. Needless to say, it was a joyous occasion for us all as we hadn't known how she and the rest of the family had fared. (She had been in contact with my other son in nearby Slidell, and they were fine.)

We returned to our house to check the damage and start cleaning up and found mud everywhere. One of the most emotional and difficult things I have ever had to do was to pull out our belongings and furniture that had been in the family for years and throw it in a junk pile on the street. We had lived in Waveland for twenty-four years, and much of our furniture and knickknacks had been in our families for years before then. After that came the destruction phase—pulling out wet

Sheetrock, ripping up the carpet, and tearing out the kitchen cabinets. After a few weeks, the interior of the house was basically empty, waiting to be rebuilt.

A few days after the storm, our neighbor Richard Hubbard got his well up and running. That meant that we could take a cold shower. It was wonderful! Then Lili and George Stahler, our across-the-street neighbors and best friends, got their well working, and we had the option of showering there. It was kind of comical to see a bunch of people with towels heading for the neighborhood showers. What a blessing! Many people were still in shock, not knowing where to turn or what to do next. No one could get in or out of Waveland or Bay St. Louis without special passes. There was no electricity or drinkable water—it was like being in a war zone.

About that time, an army of volunteers showed up on our doorsteps and began removing fallen trees from the street and on the houses. Police from Florida and Georgia and other states began patrolling on land and in the air. Electric companies from all over came to get electricity restored. At the Sav-A-Center shopping center, volunteers began distributing ice and water (which we will be eternally grateful for—you don't realize how much you miss these two items) and later food. Wal-Mart opened under a tent with real groceries. There were also people from Florida going house to house, checking on how people were doing and bringing items that they knew we needed (having gone through destructive hurricanes themselves in Florida).

The first really memorable and uplifting event took place the Sunday after the storm with the mass at St. Rose de Lima in Bay St. Louis with Bishop Thomas Rodi. People knew at that time that there was a light at the end of the tunnel and hope for recovery.

The second event was the mass at St. Clare where a tent

(which is still being used today) had been donated by a Canadian gentleman. It was erected on the site of the old church, and it was overflowing with parishioners outside in the front of the church and outside behind the altar. There were not many dry eyes that day.

After a month, things were made somewhat bearable. Churches in the area were starting to get organized and evaluating what was needed to help people to get their lives back together and to get them back in their homes.

St. Clare School re-opened, thanks to the efforts of the principal, Mark Cumella and Father Gillespie, and donations from people, parishes, and schools from all over the country. This was a huge lift for the spirits of the St. Clare family. Unfortunately, it had already been decided by the Diocese that it would have to close its doors at the end of 2006 and merge with Bay Catholic School, with a new name "Holy Trinity School" under three parishes: Our Lady of the Gulf, St. Rose de Lima, and St. Clare.

St. Bartholomew's Catholic Church in Indianapolis made a monetary commitment to help start and sustain St. Clare's recovery, and they sent Jane Crady to help coordinate our efforts. She really got everything off the ground and showed us how to keep it going after she left. Father Gillespie went to St. Pat's in Chicago to meet with their Harbor of Hope members. They also made a commitment to support our recovery efforts with volunteers and funds. Both St. Bart's and St. Pat's have helped us with funds, volunteers, and prayers. There were many other churches of all different denominations who supported us in our recovery.

In October, November, and December of 2005, volunteers began pouring into Waveland and Bay St Louis, bringing with them the skills to help rebuild our cities. Our job in recovery was to coordinate the volunteers with the houses needing repairs and make sure the materials were there so the work would not be delayed. The first phase was to gut houses - this phase is when non-skilled labor was utilized. Many church groups, civic organizations, and youth groups (wonderful giving people) came from all over the country, working from daybreak to dark. There were so many groups I couldn't begin to tell you where they were all from. Some of these groups have been coming back year after year. One group that comes to mind was headed up by Betty Fisher from Minnesota. Many of these people have become friends for life. I thank God for these wonderful people.

After the first year or so, the next phase began—getting people back into their homes. I do not know how many people St. Rose put back in to their homes. I am sure it was a large number. To date, St. Clare has helped 343 families get back into their homes.

The help we received from so many churches, grants, and donations was just unbelievable. So many individuals sent checks on a regular basis, and they are still coming in to assist in our effort to help others. So many lives were touched by these angels sent to help us that there is no way to thank them for their sacrifices, but they will always be in my prayers.

Betsy and I have been back in our house for four years now, but we still have a work in progress. It's taken St. Clare three and a half years to get the new church and parish hall started. We are expecting to dedicate the new church and parish hall in early September 2010—five years after Katrina.

May God bless all who have helped in our recovery and prayed for us.

Noel Phillips was born in New Orleans, LA. He has been married to Betsy for 38 years and they have 3 children and 7 grandchildren. They have been living in Waveland, MS for the last 31 years. He owned and operated his own business and currently spends his retirement working for his home church, St. Clare in Waveland, MS.

Making Us

Philip Williams

I was born in Bay St. Louis, Mississippi, but lived in San Antonio, Washington DC, and Los Angeles for the greater part of my life. I returned to Bay St. Louis in 1980 and married Beverly Dedeaux from Pass Christian, Mississippi. We have been blessed with three daughters.

When Katrina was forecasted, most felt it was going to be a small storm with little or no consequence. Therefore, very little preparation was made initially for what turned out to be a disaster. What a shock we received! Katrina ended up being one of the worst storms in United States history.

Beverly's family lives in DeLisle, Mississippi, which is located eight to ten miles north of Bay St. Louis. DeLisle is considered to be higher and drier land compared to Bay St Louis, thus not prone to flooding. My wife and family chose to stay there with her family to ride the storm out. I chose to stay at the homestead on Old Spanish Trail.

While we still had hot water, I took a good hot shower and flung myself across the bed in my boxer shorts. The winds began to blow. Gradually they got stronger. Every now and then I would hear pieces of tin blowing around, then boards, then tree limbs. I got out of bed and began to pray, "Oh Lord, help Your child." Moments later I heard glass breaking in our bedroom facing the east. The entire window was being blown out pane by pane. At this time we were enduring the maximum wind speed, and windows in other rooms began to blow out. I tried to stack furniture against the windows, but it did not help. Within minutes, all the windows in the house were blown away. I looked at the two-story commercial building next to my house; the entire second floor was blowing away one side at a time. Its length was one hundred feet, and the second floor was completely swept away. Across the street lived an old lady, Miss Rosie. I witnessed all of her walls cave in and prayed she was not trapped in the collapsed house.

Frightened, I ran out of the house and leaned against our cinder block wall facing the wind. I managed to fight the wind and pick up an eight foot catering table and leaned it on the cinder blocks in front of me. There I was, between the table and the wall in my boxers, which were sliding off my body. I was too busy holding on to the table to grab them, so they fell to the ground. So there I was standing naked. To make matters worse, there was rising water all around me, and the red ants that were floating began crawling up onto my legs. I withstood the pain and tried to shake them off. I began to pray again and again, "Lord, if You take my life, please don't let it be painful." When you face such a helpless situation, your thoughts race from one thing in life to the next. Most of all I was remembering and praying for my lovely wife and beautiful children. I stayed in that position for a little over an hour, praying and hoping that we would all make it through alive.

Immediately after the storm, it was time to find out about the safety and security of family members. I had been praying that they were safe and secure. My heart is filled with gratitude to this day that all my loved ones for whom I prayed ceaselessly survived this monstrous storm. In the midst of so much suffering, beautiful things began to happen. I had never imagined that I would ever see a time when blacks, whites, Jews, Asians, Indians, low class, and high class would come together as one. Neither money nor political pull, nor status made a difference. We all prayed and acted as one during those crucial hours of darkness, thirst, hunger and sadness. In the long lines for water and ice stood political adversaries, bankers, judges, and their children; all were there for a drink of cool, clean water. The emergency hot food tent operators received no complaints regarding the taste or quality of food served. We were all very happy for whatever we were blessed with.

Our home suffered severe wind damage. However, my wife and three girls were spared any physical injury. This had to be by the grace of God. We were also grateful when we discovered that our church, St. Rose de Lima, was still standing, basically untouched by the floodwaters.

Fr. Sebastian immediately stepped up to lead the church in the recovery efforts. The first Mass celebrated by Bishop Thomas Rodi gave all who gathered there a sense of hope and comfort. Our church parish became the focal point for food distribution, clothing, financial aid, spiritual advice, trauma conciliation, and a worldwide volunteer recruitment and displacement center. This was truly a time when town folk and parish members were really pulling together.

When my wife, Beverly, and I looked around, we realized we were seriously blessed compared to many others in the county. Beverly began working at St. Rose Center, sorting and distributing clothing. I began working with our Diocese of Biloxi as a housing reconstruction specialist. We gave thanks to the Lord, put our own repairs on the back burner, and took one day at a time.

As time passed, we felt we were blessed daily with love from the community and from the volunteers. We were also blessed with financial contributions and building supplies. Our home presently is 99.5 percent complete, and that's good enough for me. The remaining .5 percent can fall under "general maintenance."

Upon his arrival at St. Rose a few years before, Fr. Sebastian had suggested the men of the parish form a choir. That was the beginning of the St. Rose Gospel Male Ensemble. (We did, however, have a few ladies working with us; so we changed the name to become the St. Rose Gospel Ensemble.) We wanted to build a name for ourselves distinct from the well-known St. Rose Gospel Choir. We started off with three members and soon the number increased to ten. Presently, we have a membership of twenty-eight. The membership consists of retired educators, trade professionals, retirees, military, law enforcement, and ordinary everyday folk worshiping and praising the Lord through song. The impact of the storm was felt by each and every one of the Ensemble members. When given the opportunity, we were able to gather to record a number of storm-related songs. We recently released our CD entitled, *Lord, You Pulled Us Through*. And He certainly did.

The Katrina experience has brought my family and me closer to Christ and to one another. The lessons of endurance, hope, love, compassion, and faith will continue to form our lives in this beautiful community.

Now that the storm is over, and many of us have recovered, what I really miss most is the togetherness we shared as one people. As new trials face the Gulf Coast, such as the recent oil disaster, I hope we remember the lessons of Katrina … I hope we remember to pull together as one to tackle any new Coast challenges that come our way. And when they come, I just wonder if the Lord is trying to tell us something, or if it's His way to get us to love one another more.

Philip Williams, a local business owner, lives with his wife Beverly and three children in Bay St. Louis, MS. From 1980 to 2005 he owned and operated Williams Pit BBQ Restaurant, Williams Distribution and Supply, and Williams Auto Restoration. He has served both civic and church community in manifold ways.

God Helps Those Who Help Themselves
Ames Kergosien

Being a lifelong resident of Bay St. Louis since 1940, I have experienced several storms and hurricanes. I pride myself to be part of the fourth generation of the family who arrived from Brittany, France.

I can remember five major hurricanes that affected our area. The first was in 1947; two were very severe but not nearly as severe and damaging as Hurricane Katrina. At the time of Hurricane Katrina, four of my six children and their families lived on the Gulf Coast. Two were in Bay St. Louis, and two were in Pass Christian. One in Bay St. Louis had severe damage to the house, another in Bay St. Louis completely lost their dwelling, and the two in Pass Christian lost their homes and possessions.

During Hurricane Katrina, my youngest daughter Ellen and her family stayed with me as I live on some of the high ground in Bay St. Louis. She was scheduled to be in the hospital the day after Katrina to have a baby and could not have natural childbirth. We were ready for the wind, but none of us in our wildest dreams expected any flooding where we lived. As the water started rising in my house, we quickly raised furniture and personal property. It really scared me as my floor level is twenty-eight feet above sea level! My greatest fear was if my daughter would go into labor, leaving us totally helpless. But God was there!

There was thirty inches of water in the house and severe damage to roof and windows. That afternoon, my daughter's doctor (who lived two blocks away from the house) managed to come to my house. She recounted to us that she had to carefully walk in between the fallen power lines, trees, and debris. It was indeed a great relief to all of us to see her there with Ellen. I was truly touched by the kindness of this wonderful doctor, who cared for her patient even when all were faced with the storm's devastation. She was very emphatic that we needed to get Ellen to a hospital as soon as possible. She suggested Baton Rouge, as our hospital was under water. Though we did not know the extent of the damage in New Orleans at that time, we knew that city was not an option as they were under mandatory evacuation.

All of our vehicles had been destroyed. The thought of getting Ellen to the hospital was frightening, yet we knew we had no other choice. People all say that they lost cell phone connections. I do not know how, but my call to my cousin who lived in the northern part of Hancock County went through! He agreed to meet us out on the highway because there was little possibility of getting much closer to the house due to the trees and debris on the streets. We walked a long way to get to the car, and we took a long slow drive to Baton Rouge. I really admire Ellen's courage and the calmness of my son-in-law, Bill Beckham. The next day she gave birth to a beautiful baby girl whom they named Caroline.

My real estate office on U.S. 90 close to the Bay Bridge was completely destroyed, and nothing was found. After Katrina, there was no transportation, no groceries, etc. After several days, a group from California (Calvary Chapel) set up a food service place next to the football stadium and served three hot meals a day to the public. I can only thank God for the gracious volunteers, their good food, and their caring service to hundreds of people. I remember vividly how gracefully they prepared and served food on Thanksgiving Day by the Train Depot.

We had many volunteers from all over the United States who came in and helped people clean up, repair, and replace homes. We could not have made it if not for the many volunteers. Many people, including my children, were able to repair and re-build with their help.

My son who lived in Alexandria, Louisiana, came with blue tarps, and we had a temporary roof two days after Katrina. God has given me a hard-working spirit, and I try to use all my abilities in difficult situations. I thank God for the ability He gave me to gut the house the week after the storm and begin repairs. I may have been the first homeowner in Bay St. Louis to gut the house. I have always been a firm believer that God helps those who help themselves.

Yes, we all needed help! But there were some who tried to abuse the generosity and goodwill of the people and churches. It did aggravate me to see some people sitting back and doing practically nothing to better their condition. They seemed to be expecting the government and volunteers to assist and finance them. However, I can say these small aggravations were nothing in comparison to the goodness that was radiating in our community.

Katrina was so devastating; I knew so many people needed help and assistance. Thousands of families had lost their homes. Although my house was severely damaged, the structure was still sound. In the weeks, months, and years after the storm, countless volunteers from all over the country were in our city, giving us a hand when we couldn't do it on our own. I joined the St. Rose Task Force and helped with the relief and recovery efforts spearheaded by my church. That was my way of showing gratitude and appreciation for the blessings we received.

Ames Kergosien is a lifelong resident of Bay St. Louis. He owned and operated a real estate business for over four decades. Currently he is part of several civic and church organizations. He also loves to spend time with his family and friends in this wonderful town he loves dearly.

Hope in the Midst of Tragedy

Fr. Jaison Mangalath, SVD

When Hurricane Katrina devastated the Gulf Coast, I was in Baton Rouge, Louisiana, serving as the pastor of St. Paul the Apostle Catholic Church. I was anxious, like everyone else, about the devastation it was about to cause on the residents of the Gulf Coast. I was particularly concerned about the welfare of the elderly and retired priests and brothers of St. Augustine's residence in Bay St. Louis. I was in communication with Fr. Sebastian Myladiyil, my seminary classmate and friend who at that time was the pastor of St. Rose De Lima Church in Bay St Louis. Since there was an evacuation notice, I invited him to come and stay with me in Baton Rouge for the duration of the hurricane. He set out for Baton Rouge rather late on Sunday afternoon, only to find out that he could not head anywhere but north. He eventually turned around and made his way back to Bay St. Louis where he stayed put with the rest of the residents of St. Augustine's and lived through the horror of this terrible hurricane.

My last communication with Fr. Sebastian was in the early morning of August 29, 2005. That connection was lost as the winds of Katrina gained speed. I was deeply alarmed by the fact that I had no way of knowing what was happening to my dear friend and to the community of St. Augustine, and of course, to the many people I had come to know through my association with the church community of St. Rose. Nevertheless, I remained prayerful, hoping for the best and continued trying to reach Fr. Sebastian many times. Even after the hurricane had passed, I could not reach him. I was deeply worried about the situation until I got a call from him that lasted for a few seconds. I was very relieved he and I were finally able to connect, especially after numerous failed attempts. Gratefully, he was very much alive and in fact, was on an almost epic journey in an old church van transporting elderly priests to a safer location in Vicksburg, Mississippi. As I later discovered, the episodes from that journey in itself resonated with courage, adventure, and humor, which became commonalities in spirit and faith among those who had now begun to come together in the midst of the devastation.

Fr. Sebastian gave me a sense of how they had survived through the hurricane. He also related to me the extent of damage caused by wind and floodwaters. As buildings flooded, some of those who occupied the Retreat House had to swim across to get to the safer grounds of St. Augustine's Residence. The Residence itself was flooded on the ground level. Everything touched by the floodwaters was ruined and life as we/they knew it was brought to a total halt. I felt a sense of urgency to reach out and help. With a keen sense of my own gratitude for being spared from the impact of Katrina, I embarked upon a personal journey to lend a hand. I began by making many trips to Bay St. Louis in the weeks following the hurricane and had many opportunities to witness the efforts toward recovery and rebuilding. My first trip was only two days after the hurricane, which was the earliest day I could get any access to that location. I recall very vividly driving down I-12 and then I-10, not seeing any vehicle at all, except a border patrol vehicle. Along the way, as I passed Hammond, Louisiana, there were visible signs of devastation and destruction—boats laid out on the side of the interstate that you wouldn't see every day; high waters and fallen trees; vehicles submerged in water littered the highway; and sections of the woods near Pearl River were ripped apart, left as evidence of a strong tornado produced by the high winds of Katrina.

Finally when I arrived at St. Augustine's, I was greeted by a few residents and other local residents who had sought refuge there. Among them was a little boy who was anxiously waiting for his dad to come to see him. As I tried to make small conversation with him, his eyes remained fixed on the horizon in eager expectation. There was a profound silence all around as people gathered in small groups. It was quite evident that they were still trying to grasp the reality of what had just happened. Even as they greeted me with a warm smile, I sensed the numbness that they felt within. Their lives were changed forever! No one seemed to know what the next course of action was. Thankfully, St. Augustine's became an early hub of hope and safety. It offered them a place to gather, share their feelings, and console one another. Even as early as then, there was another group of people busying themselves in cleaning and pulling out carpets from rooms flooded by the high waters of Katrina. I unloaded my van that I had filled with water, fuel, and a few other necessities, only to realize how little it was compared to the immense need of the people who had lost everything. I returned home that afternoon with a few of the elderly priests who needed to be transported to safer locations.

I made several more trips to Bay St. Louis, bringing supplies and volunteers from my church and from Our Lady of Mercy parish in Baton Rouge. While delivering the homily one morning during Mass at Our Lady of Mercy Church, I shared my experiences of assisting in Bay St. Louis. After the Mass, people gave me donations to purchase supplies and fuel. Among them were Mrs. Donna Hall and her two daughters. Donna informed me that her husband Robert was a jack-of-all-trades and that she was going to recruit him to go with me to Bay St. Louis. Robert and I made the next trip together, and he was able to patch up the roof of St. Rose de Lima Church to minimize damage from further leaking. Donna volunteered to do the laundry that I brought back, and she also volunteered to do some shopping. It was absolutely amazing how grace, mercy, and compassion flowed from the congregation of the church, both at St. Paul and at Our Lady of Mercy. It inspired people to take action and extend a helping hand to those who may have been so paralyzed by what had happened to them, and by the devastation and destruction surrounding them, that helping themselves seemed impossible.

The following week, I took my youth group and other volunteers from St. Paul's on my trip. This trip was also one of the most outstanding moments of time stored in my memory; it played out as a catalyst for all the good that would come out of the devastation that was sweeping the Coast. My youth group and other volunteers eagerly arrived to begin working. While the adult volunteers busied themselves at St. Augustine's, the youth busied themselves at St. Rose de Lima Parish to help clean up the church and the school building so that a relief location could be opened. While the youth were cleaning the inside, Fr. Sebastian and I ventured outside to clean the debris from fallen trees in front of the church. While we were busy at this task, a stranger stopped and visited with us. He said he was dispatched by his pastor to find out what could be done to help in the recovery efforts. He pulled out a large bundle of cash that his pastor had sent and told Fr. Sebastian to do whatever he thought was necessary to help the people. He explained why he decided to give us that money—he said he had been scouting the area for the past few days looking for signs of hope. In the midst of devastation, he wanted to see people engaged in positive action that would work as a catalyst for the recovery of this region. When he came around the area where we were working, he witnessed what he was looking for. We had men, women, and children working to begin anew. He saw signs of hope that assured him that Hurricane Katrina was not powerful enough to destroy the audacity of human will to find hope in the midst of tragedy. The stranger gave the money with the assurance of returning soon with more help and walked away.

One of the things I wondered about in the days following the devastation was why God preserved St. Rose and its campus from wind and flood damage. After this incident, I had my answer. God always preserves a remnant so that, even when everything else is destroyed, a new hope can sprout, take root, and grow to renew the face of the earth. The recovery efforts that St. Rose has spearheaded since brought meaning and purpose to the lives of many. They gave signs of vitality and resilience and encouraged people to return home and strengthen their bonds and start their lives again. In all of my experiences, this one simple incident stands out as the most striking, because it speaks about what was most important in all such situations, which is hope—it never disappoints.

In the wake of the devastation left by Hurricane Katrina, I am sure that many human relationships were changed and deepened. Many may have looked at their relationships in a new light and with a new appreciation. One of my important growths through Katrina was to add a new depth and meaning to my friendship with Fr. Sebastian. My friendship with him goes back to 1987 when we both entered seminary with the Society of the Divine Word at St. John's Mission Seminary, Changanacherry, Kerala in India. We had both completed our tenth grade at that time. We met for the first time in the seminary and during the next twelve years, we fostered a relationship, which bloomed into a wonderful and trusting friendship that would endure through our ordination to priesthood in 1999 and through our journey to the United States of America. We were assigned to parishes in neighboring cities in Louisiana—he at St. Edward's Church in New Iberia, and I at Immaculate Heart of Mary Church in Lafayette. It was our mutual support and many deep conversations that helped us to transition well in the first few years of life in this new world. We discovered things together and understood the culture together. Sometimes we laughed at ourselves and teased one another. We learned to play tennis together and to eat at fast-food restaurants without letting the cashier discover our ignorance about the fast-food culture and language. We looked forward to our days off to spend time in fun and conversation. We traveled together and shared our hopes and dreams, enjoying a mutual sense of brotherhood.

Katrina brought a huge interruption to this time we spent together. In the weeks and months and even years past Katrina, I am still looking forward to the time when he and I can spend those good old days together. Fr. Sebastian spearheaded the recovery efforts in Bay St. Louis and became so involved with the work that visiting or calling him was no longer the same; the work and the meetings demanded his time and attention. When I visited him, I was often forced to spend time alone when he was away in a meeting or when frequent phone calls from volunteers or agencies interrupted our conversation. During those moments, I missed the good old days with my friend and I sometimes felt agitated by the constant interruptions when we would finally sit down for a meal or for a good, deep conversation. At those moments, I recognized that our friendship demanded new growth and dimension. Katrina had redefined our focus and the way we were to maintain our friendship. It demanded a greater generosity and understanding from me. I could no longer expect the same Fr. Sebastian. His ministry demanded a new kind of leader, and I had to accept and support it just as much as I enjoyed and supported our old way of being friends. And that is what I did. As a result, our conversations took on another depth and meaning. We talked about his ministry and projects. He told me all about how he could now repair roofs and paint walls and rip apart Sheetrock walls and replace them with ease. I in turn critiqued his style and involvement, walked with him as he led his people from the front lines, and offered words of consolation and comfort at the first anniversary prayer service of Katrina that was held at St. Rose de Lima Church. I was there proudly supporting him when he was chosen to be one of the outstanding citizens of Hancock County and then when he made his trip to Washington, D.C. to make presentations to different leaders. Today, because of these experiences, we have a deeper sense of gratitude for one another and a deeper bond of friendship.

Of all things, Katrina gave us (forced on us) the opportunity to reevaluate our priorities in life, to appreciate relationships in a new light, and to become more aware of the fragility of human achievement. Then finally, we realized, the only lasting things are those that are built in the human spirit—surrender, faith, hope, and love, even in the midst of tragedy.

Fr. Jaison Mangalath, SVD is a Divine Word Missionary priest from India, working in the United States since 1999. In 2001, he was appointed as Pastor of St. Paul the Apostle Church in Baton Rouge, LA. Besides his pastoral duties, he served on several important committees in the diocese of Baton Rouge. Currently he serves as pastor of Holy Ghost Catholic Church, Opelousas, LA. He became a US citizen on January 7, 2010.

Quiet Life Blown Away ... But Still Grateful
Clementine Williams

My life as I had known it for sixty-four years was completely shattered on August 29, 2005 when Hurricane Katrina came on the shores of my hometown, Bay St. Louis.

I am Clementine Williams, the oldest daughter of the six girls born to our wonderful and caring parents, Douglas and Louise Williams. My parents, now deceased, completed their high school education at St. Rose de Lima. Even though they did not attend college, they wanted the best for their daughters (Clementine, the late Rosine, Susan, Pamela, Donna, and Noella). They did just that. After I graduated from St. Rose de Lima, I attended several universities, including Alcorn State, Tennessee State, and the University of Southern Mississippi, receiving several degrees. My career was in education, and I worked forty years as a teacher and school administrator. My life revolved around the classrooms of several districts in Mississippi, and I failed to acquire a husband and children; however, I feel blessed because I touched the lives of over one thousand children and still hear from many of them.

In 2001, the year before I retired, I had my home remodeled, wanting to have a place to sit back and relax in a home that was all paid for. All that was for naught when Hurricane Katrina entered our Hancock County with a furor that had no mercy on many families, their homes, businesses, and property. My sisters, my niece and her family, and I left the day before the storm heading north to our sister Donna's home in Clinton, Mississippi. On our return, we could see places ravished by the storm long before we reached our houses. Trees were down everywhere. Homes were completely destroyed, and automobiles had been drenched in water; animals were dead along roadways, and boats were washed up on land and sometimes in the middle of the road.

Even though a tree had fallen on my house, it was still standing. On entering, I was overwhelmed and distraught at what was before me. The water in my home had receded, but everything from twenty-five to thirty inches high on down was ruined. My relatively newly re-modeled home was in ruins. I was devastated and sat on the porch for an hour or two and cried. After crying awhile, I began to realize at least my house was still standing, while the homes of many family members and neighbors were totally destroyed. The greatest gift of all was the fact that we all were alive. We soon began to lean on each other for strength, courage, and a whole lot of hope.

As I walked and drove through the community, I saw that my church, St. Rose de Lima, and my school were still standing as a beacon of faith in our community. Mass was held there by the bishop on the first Sunday after the storm. What a blessing to all of us! St. Rose became a distribution center, a place to pray and vent if need be, and a place for volunteers to stay as they came in from all over the country to help families rebuild. We had an inspiring pastor, and under his guidance the St. Rose Outreach And Recovery (SOAR) project was organized. This organization of parishioners, volunteers, and friends was respon-sible for roofing, rebuilding homes, and providing services to hundreds of families in the county, including me. These are the people who kept me motivated. I had complained of backaches for several years, but during this time of cleaning out my home, helping serve food to many, providing water to volunteers, I had no time for aches and pain. My church, family, neighbors, and friends kept me in survival mode. I will be forever grateful to the wonderful and caring volunteers who helped not only me but also people throughout the entire community.

While volunteer assistance was ever present, I had the diffi-cult task of trying to convince my insurance company of many years to pay for the damages to my home. Dealing with them and having to go to mediation with them for just a pittance of help was the hardest thing I had to deal with. My home was in shambles, and I had to beg for the insurance funds that I felt were due to me.

As I reflect on the tragedy that occurred, I must also reflect on all the good that developed as family, neighbors, and the many volunteers bonded in love and respect for life. I realize the miracle of it all was the closeness and love of strangers that per-meated throughout my being. I remember on my second day of clearing the mud out of my home, a complete stranger stopped. She had a van full of cases of water and had come from Colorado; she said bringing water was all she could do. She gave me a case and began helping to pull carpet and soggy furniture out of my home. She was the most cheerful and upbeat person I had seen in a while—truly a godsend.

The miracles continued. Money became a problem because, before an insurance settlement and a possible homeowners grant, I had dipped deeply into savings for materials and sup-plies, leaving no money for contractors. SOAR and Eight Days of Hope and several other volunteers provided much needed help. I was more than willing to sit at Eight Days of Hope's headquarters at St. Rose taking phone calls and assisting the volunteers in charge. It was a blessing to give back.

After fourteen months in my FEMA trailer (which was known as the "Bungalow" in the neighborhood), I was able to move into my home in December 2006. Even though I had re-tired in 2002, I was able to work part-time as an educational consultant. This work allowed me the ability to refurnish my home.

I am so very grateful for all the kindnesses shown to me and I am most thankful that, through the example of the goodness of others, I now give more freely and joyfully to organizations and charities that help victims when a disaster strikes. God is good ... and through His grace I am truly on my way to complete recovery.

Clementine Williams is a native of Bay St. Louis and lifelong member of St. Rose de Lima church. She worked as an educator and school principal for over 40 years before retiring from Pass Christian School District. She continues to be active in civic and church organizations.

"Come This Far by Faith"

Dianne Frederick

I am a mother of five children—Robert, Chianti, Natalie, Nakira and Cassie—and grandmother of eight. I pride myself in being a dedicated worker and I feel blessed to be devoted to my church. On August 29, 2005, Hurricane Katrina came into our town unwelcomed, delivering a powerful punch that would go down in history and reshape this small city we call home.

On the evening of the storm, the weather report was not looking good. I had to decide whether to evacuate with my children to Georgia or stay with my husband, Allen, who was at the time in the hospital in Gulfport, Mississippi. He had been there since June 14, 2005. Allen had a blockage in four of his arteries that caused him to have major heart surgery. After three weeks, he came home for less than a day before returning to the hospital. We were told he needed another surgery, a thoracotomy, which eventually complicated his condition. He was paralyzed from his chest down. After some thought, my inner being said, "In sickness and in health, until death do us part"; so my decision was to stay with my husband at the hospital.

I was told if I stayed at the hospital, I couldn't leave until the hurricane was over. I had to wear a hospital band on my arm for identification in case the worst were to happen. Soon we began to witness the fury of the Mother Nature. Windows were blown out, and the first floor took in some water. We were all in the hallways praying and hoping for the best.

Katrina beat on coastal communities until she got tired. Then she left, leaving us with death all around and millions of dollars of destruction. I remember looking out the window of the fifth floor of the hospital, which is located about a mile from the shore, and seeing nothing but the beach. Every other building that was there prior to Katrina was gone.

Two days later, I still had no contact with my children who were in Augusta, Georgia, with relatives. On day three, non-patients could leave. It took two hours to get to Bay St. Louis from Gulfport, which is normally only a twenty minute drive. Along the road were dead animals and tons of twisted debris. I finally reached home to find a large seventy-five-year-old tree sitting on top of the roof. The big surprise was waiting inside. I opened the door, and my two dogs ran out, happy to be alive. I noticed everything from about two feet down was wet, and all the floors were covered with mud. After surveying the damage, I went to look for my sister and brother who had decided to stay. Thank God they were okay. They told me that if I went to the old Bay Bridge that was destroyed, I might be able to pick up a signal on my cell phone to talk with my children so off I went. What a great joy to hear my children were okay!

The next day Allen was airlifted to Panama City, Florida, because the hospital in Gulfport had taken on so much damage. I traveled back and forth every week, staying weekdays in Florida. I had no job because both my day job and my night job were gone. Six months later in February 2006, I finally went back to work at my day job, driving the school bus for the local Head Start. Thank you, Jesus, I was working again because money was getting pretty low. I was beginning to think, *How am I going to keep making trips back and forth to Florida while I am on unemployment?* Thankfully, I didn't have a house note for those six months because I could not have made it. I was blessed with good friends and neighbors who kept me motivated.

When I would come home from Florida, the neighbors and I would go to Teenie Williams' house where we could laugh and have fun. She was the mother of the neighborhood. She had none by birth, but she had all of us. We nicknamed her FEMA trailer, "Teenie Bungalow." Neighbors Kelvin and Kessa called her trailer the "romper room" where all the kids could go play. We all had lost possessions, but we had friendship. Also we had our church, St. Rose. It seemed to be untouched! How could this be, if not but God's intervention? The church opened the doors of its school buildings and some families lived there until they got a place to stay. The school became a distribution center, aiding families with clothing, food, and water, as well as the Word of God. Thank you, Lord! We were beginning to see light at the end of the tunnel.

My youngest daughter, Cookie (seventeen at the time), left Augusta, Georgia, to go live with her nanny in Jacksonville, Florida, to be closer to me in Panama City, Florida. She got settled in and started school there. Sometime in December 2005, I was blessed with a FEMA trailer—home sweet home! Nanny Beth and Cookie packed up and moved home. The FEMA trailers allowed families to come back to this beautiful place we call home. St. Rose hosted volunteers who came to help us rebuild and repair our homes. I thought, "Where would they stay?" We only had a small trailer for ourselves. St. Rose and other churches provided classrooms and church halls. Some volunteers slept in tents and made use of homemade outside showers. To see volunteers from all over the world come help us was strong motivation. My heart is full of gratitude for the wonderful people who came to our aid.

I was faced with yet another trial in life just two days before the first anniversary of the storm. I had planned to add on to my house to have more space for Allen upon his return from Florida. But that was not part of God's plan. He was called to his true home by his Maker. On August 27, 2006, Allen passed away in a Florida nursing center. He had never returned home after he was airlifted to the Panama City hospital. On November 23, 2006, two of my grandchildren lost their father. My family is still facing trials. My twenty-seven-year-old daughter, Nakira, has been diabetic since the age of seven and insulin dependent. In the last five years she has been diagnosed with cerebral palsy, early signs of neuropathy, and high blood pressure. She now takes dialysis three times a week and will for the rest of her life. My prayer is that she will be able to get a kidney and pancreas transplant.

I once asked, "Why me?" and my pastor Fr. Sebastian said, "Why not you? God knows you can handle it." I guess he is right and I am handling it one day at a time. In spite of all these trials, I have truly been blessed. I have learned in times of trouble, God is always there. I have come this far by faith, and I know faith.

Dianne Frederick is a native of Bay St. Louis, MS. She takes great pride in all the different jobs that she does. She is a committed member of St. Rose de Lima church and also volunteers her time with other churches in the area. She devotes a lot of her time to her family and friends.

Still Grieving Over a Friend

Paula Fairconnetue

I remember the week before Hurricane Katrina struck, everyone assumed that the storm would not hit anywhere in Hancock County or along the Mississippi Gulf Coast because we had been fortunate not to have had a major hurricane land for more than thirty years. The last devastating hurricane to hit was Hurricane Camille in 1969. I believe the residents of Hancock County, myself included, had become complacent, taking for granted the beauty of our little paradise on the Gulf Coast. We enjoyed the beaches and tropic-like weather. We especially enjoyed all the seafood the Gulf waters have to offer and the laid-back lifestyle that anyone could easily become accustomed to. For reasons not fully understood, many of us were not too worried about a major storm hitting our area.

Those thoughts of false security were quickly swept away once the news came that Hurricane Katrina was heading our way, packing winds of 150 miles per hour. I remember waking up on Sunday morning, August 28, 2005, with the news anchor announcing that Hurricane Katrina was a Category 5 storm, and it was heading straight to New Orleans and the Mississippi Gulf Coast. I was frightened as I heard warnings from the weather stations telling everyone to expect storm surge of thirty-five feet. I began packing to evacuate, but my husband, Nat, wanted to attend Mass at St. Rose de Lima before leaving town. We attended 7 a.m. Mass and decided to evacuate to our daughter Nadia's home in Atlanta, Georgia. We talked with family and friends to make sure they were making preparations to be safe. My niece, Tamera, and her children decided to follow us to Atlanta. The traffic was terrible. The regular six-hour trip to Atlanta took us eleven hours to make it to our daughter's home. We almost turned around several times to take our chances at staying at home, but the cars on the interstate were bumper-to-bumper, so we had to go with the flow.

We prayed and hoped for the best for everyone. We watched in horror at reports of Katrina unleashing her fury on the Gulf Coast. There was no way of knowing the extent of the damage and the whereabouts of people. I felt helpless many a time as I sat and imagined the worst happening. There were several occasions I asked God to calm my fears. We knew that it was futile to return to our home immediately. Under normal circumstances, a visit to see my daughter and her family was so joyful that I used to feel time rushing by me. However, this time the two-week stay at her home felt like two years away from my home. I ached to get back, but was unable to.

We returned after those two weeks to witness devastation that was even beyond our imagination. We could not believe what our eyes were seeing. We felt a sense of loss, a sense of helplessness, and a sense of fear of the future as we looked around our once beautiful home, our neighborhood, and our city. The hard part was seeing our home for the first time. Everything was destroyed; the ceilings of our home had collapsed in several places, scattering insulation and debris everywhere. Although our home was not flooded, the walls, wooden flooring, and all our possessions were destroyed from rainwater that had come through the open roof. However, we counted our blessings because the structure of the home was still sound. There were so many people whose homes were completely destroyed or washed away.

The most devastating part of the storm for me was not losing material possessions, but the deaths of a lifelong friend/classmate Kim Bell and her son. Kim and I were good friends from the time my family and I moved to Bay St. Louis in 1964 until the day she died. It's still hard for me to understand why she had decided to stay in her home, which was located two blocks from the beach, when the weather stations and local emergency agencies pleaded with everyone to evacuate. Kim was a good person. I truly miss her. She and her only child lost their lives in the storm, but my faith assures me that they are in a better place.

I'll never forget waiting in long lines in ninety-eight degree weather to get assistance. Our lives consisted of waiting in lines for water, for food, for medical attention, for insurance, and for FEMA assistance. Our lives had turned upside down. Normalcy seemed to have been washed away with the storm waters.

It took us just about a whole year to repair and renovate our home. It was the longest year of our lives. Again, we were fortunate that we didn't have some of the bad experiences other people were having with contractors taking their money and skipping town. Stories were spreading about contractor fraud everywhere. We were blessed in so many ways.

When I look back at the months and years since Katrina, I can honestly say that I have seen and been touched by the goodness of people who came from everywhere to help us. My Katrina experience gave me profound insights. It revealed to me that in a world that is often portrayed as negative and violent, there are so many good people and so much good that is present in our world.

Paula and her husband Nathaniel Fairconnetue have been married for thirty-five years and are proud parents of three children: Natalie, Nadia, and Nathaniel, Jr., and grandparents of three wonderful boys. She has been a faithful city worker of Bay St. Louis, MS and gives her time and talents generously to St. Rose Church.

Prayers Go Up, Blessings Come Down

Tamera Labat Whavers

The year 2005 is one that my family will never forget. On April 20, 2005, my husband surrendered himself to the Federal Bureau of Prisons in Beaumont, Texas where he was sentenced to serve twelve years in federal prison. I was terrified at the thought of being a single parent raising three children: Raven (14), Aaron Jr. (7), and Dillon (6). I have always had a fear of failure, but the fear of not being able to take care of them financially nearly overwhelmed me.

That August weekend was very busy for us. At that time I was employed as a teacher's assistant at Hancock North Central Elementary School. At 3:00 on that Friday (August 26) when the end of the day school bell rang, I went to the teacher's lounge where I overheard some of the teachers talking about a tropical storm that had hit southern Florida and was now headed into the Gulf. I have always said that I would never want to live in Florida because they were always getting hit by hurricanes.

We rose early the next morning on August 27, leaving about 3:00 a.m. to visit Aaron in Beaumont, Texas. We visited with him until 3:00 that afternoon and had not thought anything about the storm. I called my mother to let her know that we were heading back home. I asked her what the situation was with the storm. She said that it was too soon to tell. My first thought was to just stay in Texas; but since I was in my mother's vehicle, I decided to head on home. We arrived home about 9:30 that night. I was exhausted and went straight to bed.

I woke up Sunday morning about 6:30 to get ready for church. I had no idea what was going on in the Gulf of Mexico

155

until my mother-in-law called and asked if I were going to evacuate because the storm was a Category 5 and headed in our direction. I was not prepared for a hurricane. On the drive from Texas, I had stopped at Wal-Mart in Crowley, Louisiana, to get some things for the hurricane, but they were getting prepared for the storm as well and their store shelves were almost bare. I didn't know what to do. I only had three hundred dollars to my name and didn't know where to go. I was really wishing I had stayed in Texas. I thought about my cousin in Mobile, Alabama, but when I called her she told me she had already evacuated to Atlanta, Georgia. A light bulb went off; my cousin, Nadia Smith, lives in Atlanta. I immediately called my aunt, Paula Fairconnetue, to see what she and her husband Nathaniel were doing as far as evacuating. She told me that they were going to Nadia's place in Atlanta, and we could come with them. I then called my mother-in-law and told her to get ready because we were going to Atlanta. But she had decided to go with her other daughter-in-law, and they were still trying to decide what to do because Pass Christian was under mandatory evacuation. To my surprise, she told me that she was not going to Atlanta because her daughter Araina didn't want to leave, stating that she only had enough money to pay the house note for that month. I told her that with a Category 5 storm she needed to get her kids and leave because she might not have a house to come back to! It was to no avail; they decided not to leave Pass Christian.

I was in a frenzy. I did not know what to do. I did not have much money; my van was not running well; and on top of all that, I was exhausted from having traveled ten hours the day before. I prayed about it and got some clothes together for a few days. I called my Aunt Paula, and she said they had already left and were on their way to Atlanta. I told her we would be coming behind them. Before we left I tried to tidy up some things around the house, and then I thought, "For what?" By that time, it was 11:00 a.m. I told the kids, "Let's go!" We piled into the van and asked God to watch over our house. As I was backing out of the driveway something struck my mind telling me to leave the key to the house for Ms. Jackie, my mother-in-law. So I called her and told her that the key to the house would be under the steps if she decided to go there. As I got onto the interstate, I thought, *Yes, no traffic!*; but not for long. I only got as far as Gulfport Exit 34, and then it was bumper to bumper from there to northern Alabama. We made it to my cousin's house at 10:00 p.m. It took eleven hours to travel what would normally take only six hours. By the time we reached Atlanta, I could barely see straight.

The night had come and gone. All we could do was wonder what was going on at home and pray that everything would be okay. The next morning we sat helplessly, watching the television and seeing that the storm was making landfall right near our home. I was able to speak with Ms. Jackie briefly before we lost communication and found out that she did go to my house and Araina and her children went to a friend's house in DeLisle, Mississippi. We lost any kind of signal we had to be able to reach someone and find out if they were okay. After a while we realized that we could send and receive text messages. We were told that we should not try to come back anytime soon because there was nothing there. We ended up staying in Atlanta for two more weeks.

After two weeks, many thoughts ran through my mind on the ride home. We had heard so many different stories about what was going on. I was told that my house only seemed to have roof damage, but when I tried to unlock the side door, my key wouldn't turn so I went to the front door. When we walked in the house we were shocked to see that our ceilings had caved in and the wood floors had buckled. But there was much more to cause me to worry. We had lost all four of our rental income properties. That was the main source of income for my family of four since my job as a teacher's assistant did not bring in much money (and the school job was gone too). My stress and anxiety level went through the roof! It helped a little when I found out that I could have my bills deferred for three months. But I still had to find a job. I thank God for opening doors for me. I was leaving a job interview at Hancock Bank when I received a phone call from a former coworker. She asked me if I would be interested in working with the Army Corps of Engineers. She said the job would require working twelve-hour days, seven days a week for the next three months. I immediately said yes. At that point I didn't care if they were twenty-four hour shifts because I needed to work to be able to take care of my family! When prayers go up, blessings come down. But I still worried myself for no reason at all. I thought about what Fr. Sebastian said in one of his homilies one time, "Worry is like a rocking chair—it gives you something to do, but it takes you nowhere." I really tried not to worry as much, but it is just one of those things that I do. The things I did do to combat that worry was to pray and to remind myself to rely on God.

I cannot say that things were smooth sailing; by no means were they at all. Although the work with the Corp of Engineers was exhausting, it helped me take care of my family financially. I was able to receive help from my church as St. Rose sent volunteers at different times to put a new roof on my house and to do other repair work that was required. I will forever be thankful to the many volunteers who came to our aid. There were also families and churches that helped me pay for my children's education, and we formed lasting friendships. What I missed the most during those days was attending Mass, as I was working seven days a week. The job ended up lasting for four months, when I was again looking for work. God opened the door once again for me. I was hired by a construction company, the first place I had submitted my resume. After two weeks, I received my first paycheck; and even though there were several bills that I had to pay, I made a prayerful decision to donate my entire first paycheck to my church. I did that out of my profound gratitude for my God and my church. People might say I was naïve, but my experience in life has taught me that God always provides. Through these uncertain and painful moments, God has made me a stronger person who is no longer afraid to face the challenges and struggles of life. Although that fear of failure is still there, I have realized that when the trials of life knock me off my feet, I can get back up. In order to succeed in life, sometimes we have to experience failure. But that fear is no longer prevalent in my life. I am forever grateful to God for the opportunities that He has provided me—to face my fears; to grow stronger in my faith; and to be able to give back a little through my involvement in the recovery efforts of my church.

Tamera Labat Whavers is a native of Bay St. Louis, MS and has lived in Pass Christian, MS for the last sixteen years. She is an administrative assistant for a mechanical contracting company at Stennis Space Center, MS. She is a life-long member of St. Rose de Lima Parish and is part of several committees and organizations.

A Storyteller's Story

Bruce Northridge

Our Katrina gifts began before Katrina even arrived. On that Saturday (when we thought the storm was headed to Texas), we spent much of the day in Slidell enjoying a very special family moment. A brother and sister who'd been separated by adoption were able to celebrate a long-awaited reunion on the occasion of the sister's fourteenth birthday. They were reunited amidst tears of joy. We had already marked it as one of the most memorable weekends of our lives. Ah, but there was plenty more to come!

It wasn't until fairly late Saturday evening when we returned home and turned on the TV to recheck the position of the storm. The news was like a punch in the gut. The storm named Katrina had turned to the north, and it had strengthened. As a coastal resident since 1977, I had enough experience to know ... and as a scientist, I had enough knowledge to accurately assess the situation. A Class 5 hurricane heading directly for us was devastating news. I told my wife Joanne that we were going to lose the house. It was the house we had bought soon after we married in 1984. It was the house where we had raised our son. But the house was just sixty yards off the Waveland beach on a low-lying lot. The news was like a smack in the face—I knew there would be nothing left by Monday morning.

In August 2005, we were actually living at our Bed and Breakfast business just off Highway 90. We had made a family financial decision to rent our furnished beach house. Our tenant for the past year had just moved out two weeks earlier, thank God. But still, much of our furniture and many of our belongings were still at the beach house. We called family and friends that evening, asking (with great urgency) if we could borrow a truck. So many people were evacuating, we worried that this might not happen. But someone came through for us. The catch was that he was evacuating first thing Sunday morning. We borrowed the truck around midnight, drove to the beach house, and began pulling furniture and belongings out of the house and loading them onto the truck. Then we'd drive the short distance (across the tracks) to our place of business and we'd unload the truck. To make maximum use of the short time we had to use the truck, we just unloaded stuff onto the front yard of the B and B. No time to waste bringing it inside! Back to get another load at 1:00 a.m. Unload onto the front yard. Another load at 2:00 a.m. Unload onto the front yard. Another at 3:00 a.m. Another at 4:00 a.m. Not infrequently, Joanne would hold up something at the house and ask, "Shall I bring this to the truck?" My answer was the same each time—"Honey, if you ever want to see it again, put it in the truck." Another load at 5:00 a.m. Last load at 6:00 a.m., and then we returned the truck around 7:00 a.m. We were exhausted and went to lie down. As tired as we were, we could not sleep with a Class 5 hurricane bearing down on us ... and with the adrenaline pumping as high as it was. One of the most surreal images of that weekend was getting up Sunday morning with the front yard looking like we were preparing for a yard sale!

Our B and B was/is a strong well-built two-story house located a mile from the beach (north of the tracks). The storm surge from Camille had been blunted by the berm that held the railroad tracks. We felt confident we would be safe from flooding. On the other hand, we had over a dozen east-facing windows. We were worried about wind damage primarily. So we brought the "yard sale" furniture into the house ... never thinking that it would be important to bring it up to the second floor. In fact, we even took artwork off the walls, wrapped them in sheets, and placed them on the floor (so they would not fall and break). We spent nearly the entire day—as tired as we were—doing hurricane preps. I was most grateful for my son-in-law's assistance in boarding up the place. Joanne was busy inside packing. She had the TV on to listen to the news as she packed. On a frequent basis, WLOX would scroll the announcement that the place where I worked was not open as a public shelter.

Joanne would ask, "Where are we evacuating to?"

I'd say, "We're going to my office."

She'd reply, "They're not open!"

And I'd say, "We're going to my office!"

I would make that pronouncement each time with a firm voice ... but it was with feigning conviction. Using my office as a hurricane shelter had worked several times before ... but that was with just three of us (me, my wife, and my son). Joanne's elderly parents were visiting from Florida (bad timing, indeed!). That made five of us. My son-in-law helping to board up the house asked to join us. I could not refuse after all his help. And his daughter was inside helping Joanne. We were up to seven. Other family members lived close to the Bay-Waveland Yacht Club and told us throughout the day that they planned on staying. We pleaded with them to change their minds. Late in the day they finally did—daughter, son-in-law, and their three children, which increased the size of our group to twelve. "We're going to my office!" But it was spoken with even less conviction. And when they arrived, ready to go, they had my son-in-law's parents with them as well!

We arrived at the government building where I worked around twilight on Sunday. Five cars and fourteen people! The wind was beginning to blow hard. We managed to get family and belongings and supplies up to my office area (on the third/ top floor) and settled in for a restless night.

Early morning, with the wind howling full force, security personnel burst in with orders—"Everyone down to the second floor, now, now, now!" It was especially tricky, with elderly family members who could not manage the stairs, but we were, indeed, fortunate to have done so. A tornado hit the building we were in, peeling parts of the roof off! We were safe, thank God. In the daylight hours, we could see that the cars parked on the north side of the building were all damaged by the tornado. We had parked in the south parking lot. Thank God, all five of our family's cars were spared any damage!

The power of nature's fury was awesome to behold as it was happening. The aftermath? "Awesome" is not the word I choose. "Overwhelming" might be a better descriptor. The over-whelming destruction left in the wake of the storm left a pain in the pit of my stomach. How would we ever recover from all this mess?

From where we were on Monday, there was a bit of the Noah's Ark story at play. Someone would venture out (like the raven from Noah's ark) but would soon return with news that the roads were impassable. Later, another would venture out (like the dove) a little further this time. A select few from our family chose to venture forth on Tuesday morning. In our story, we call this "Recon Day." We dodged major debris on the roads to find out that Katrina had brought five feet of water to our B and B (again … who would've thought to bring all those earthly pos-sessions up to the second floor?). For our family members who were going to stay in their house near the B-W Yacht Club, we could not find a waterline because, in fact, the water had gone over the highest point of their roof! Thank God they had heeded our voices to not stay there, especially with their three children!

Days three, four, and five were focused on getting wet carpet out of the B and B. That was a paramount need in order to get ahead of the mold problem. It was two weeks before I maneuvered my way south of the tracks to witness firsthand the complete devastation of our beach property. Nothing of value was ever recovered from there. (We didn't remember until later that we had left boxes of family photos up in the attic.)

In our family story, we refer to Day six as "Reunion Day." Joanne was eager to get out from the cooped-up (but safe!) office space where we had weathered the storm and its immediate aftermath. This was a place that was clean and dry and had running water. In our non-Katrina lives, we so much take for granted how much of a luxury it is to be able to take a shower! But then, there were no communications, and Joanne was very worried that her family in Florida had no idea whether we had survived, let alone everyone's worries about her mom and dad. So she chose that day to pack family members in the van and head east on I-10 to get her mom and dad out of this disaster zone and back to their home in Tallahassee. Unbeknownst to us, of course, is that Joanne's family members in Florida had also chosen that same day to travel west to Mississippi to come find us. One of the little miracles in our family's story is that Joanne and her vanful traveling east, and Joanne's family members coming from Florida traveling west, chose to pull off at the same exit off of I-10 at the same time. What a joyous reunion that was! We all thanked God for sure.

It was quite reassuring to know that Joanne and her parents and the young ones were safe. I assumed a routine I called "reverse commuting." I'd sleep in my office; help out a bit in the cafeteria in the mornings; then drive the opposite way from what I'd done most mornings the previous twenty-eight years; work all day cleaning up the mess at the B and B; get welcome relief of water and other minimal supplies from neighbors and the Church of Latter Day Saints around the corner; and then would drive back to my office in the evening to the luxury of showers and a safe, dry sleeping bag on an air mattress. We had lost our home, and the storm had wiped out our family business; but I was aware every day that my circumstances were better than most. After eighteen days in that routine, the power was restored to our Waveland neighborhood. I chose to end my "reverse commuting" routine. Joanne and our son returned from Florida, and we were together again. Again, we had it better than most. We had a couple of rooms on the second floor on the west side of the house that were in livable condition.

Our family Katrina story includes three events I call "Cavalry Days" (as in, "Hooray! The cavalry is here to save us!"). The first was when family members (who are experienced carpenters and builders) arrived from Florida with a truck filled with tools and welcome supplies. I do believe we were the first house in Waveland to get our "blue roof" put on. And for several days, chain saws were buzzing as we tackled the challenge of many broken trees.

A second Cavalry Day occurred weeks later. We realized the necessity of having to cut out all the Sheetrock that had gotten wet. We'd been on the job less than an hour, but we were already starting to realize that this was heavy work (in ninety-degree heat), and that it would likely take several days to complete the work. Then there was a knock on the door. A group of volunteers had just pulled off the highway. Ours was the first house they'd come across, and they were looking to get some work done. I told them there were other families who were much more in need. They said that they didn't have time to go search out other projects; this was their last day on the Coast, and they wanted their last day to be productive. In the months and years that followed, it was a common discussion topic among Katrina survivors—how it was better to overcome our reluctance (our pride?) to accept help when it was offered (when God sent it!). I said, "Yes!" In came a small army of workers. Saws were buzzing; hammers were whacking; and there must have been two hundred trips carrying the Sheetrock out to the street. What might have taken several days was completed in several hours. Thank God for the Methodists from South Carolina!

A third "cavalry day" once again featured our wonderfully talented and generous family members from Florida who showed up to put the new roof on the house. What a blessing! Once again we realized our good fortune. We may well have been the first house in Waveland with a new roof.

Following all those blessings, we soon had a house that was dried in (hooray new roof!), with working air conditioning, with three working bathrooms, and with 5000 square feet of floor space (mostly bare plywood) and very little furniture. Perfect! We had the opportunity to "pay it forward" by opening up our B and B (our home) to volunteers for the next year and then some. Many came and found some floor space for their air mattresses. They thanked us profusely for being able to take showers after a day of "mucking out" a house and put up with my storytelling. It was a remarkable time.

It also happened that a meeting was announced to figure out how our church family, our St. Rose family, might organize to provide help to each other the best way possible under the conditions we were in. I attended and took notes. I had access to my computer by that time so I shared my notes via email to a number of interested persons who had not been able to attend. At the meeting the next week, Fr. Sebastian told the assembled group he was passing out minutes from the first meeting. I reached for one and was surprised to see that it was a copy of my email! And that is how I came to be the Secretary (and sometimes Chair? We weren't much for titles through those years) of the Hurricane Task Force at St. Rose that eventually became SOAR—St. Rose Outreach and Recovery.

The four years that followed were probably the most grace-filled years of my life. So many wonderful good people came to help us! Thanks to SOAR we were able to provide needed assistance to thousands of people, we were able to help hundreds get back into their homes, and we were able to help a couple dozen get into new homes. I'm grateful I got to work through SOAR and share meals with wonderful good people. I got to have their good spirits wash over me and form deep friendships with people I never would have met had it not been for Katrina. So many of them had such warm listening hearts that I was allowed to tell my story … again and again and again. What a blessing!

Bruce Northridge is a member of St. Rose, who lost his Waveland home and now lives with his wife and son in Bay St. Louis, MS. He came to Mississippi in 1977 to work as a Navy Oceanographer. Bruce helped with Katrina recovery by chairing the St. Rose Hurricane Task Force. He is actively involved in different civic and church organizations.

Reflections on Hurricane Katrina

Mary Louise Coyne

August 29, 2005 was a very bad day! Hurricane Katrina had targeted Hancock County on the Mississippi Gulf Coast as ground zero. In the days leading to the storm, we were engaged in the frenzied yet focused activities of battening down the hatches at Fr. Antone's home in Kiln, Mississippi, Jerald and Lin's Diamondhead home, and my home in Devil's Elbow on Rotten Bayou in Diamondhead, Mississippi.

We waited out the storm at Jerald and Lin's home in Hattiesburg, Mississippi, located seventy-five miles north of Hancock County. On the morning of August 29, I knew we were in big trouble when we lost electricity, and the winds were gusting and by afternoon, three trees had fallen through our safe house. I recall not wanting to imagine what was happening on the Coast and praying for the best! We relied on family from the East Coast to provide CNN updates on the status of the Gulf Coast with each report more dismal than the prior, and soon even these ceased because of powerless cell phones or downed cell towers.

Jerald and I were unable to return home for five days while search and rescue activities were conducted and highways were cleared of fallen trees. Finally, as we drove south and neared Hancock County, the destruction became more evident, and we quietly began coming to terms with the reality that nothing would still be standing.

When people ask me what I lost in Katrina, I struggle with the response because it isn't just about what I lost but what we all lost as individuals and as a community and the two are inexorably linked. On an individual level, only a fractured shell remained of my home, most of my furniture and personal belongings were destroyed and scattered outside mixed with those of my neighbors; my car had been submerged in flood waters; and my university campus housing my office, books, and research landed in the Gulf of Mexico. Jerald's house was "slabbed," and with our week-end searches over the next year we found four windows with shutters intact, one wicker chair (in use today), seven seashells from his collection, and roofing scattered over a 3/8 mile swath. Fr. Antone's house, treasured theology books, and beautiful gardens were totally flooded out.

On a community level, all of my neighbors and most of my students and faculty colleagues lost their homes; and our cities, bridges, local government, recreational areas, health clinics and hospitals, medical and legal records, schools, churches, banks, grocery stores, and gas stations were either heavily damaged, destroyed, or non-functional. Many Gulf Coast residents were displaced throughout the country; while some returned after months or years, others chose never to return or rebuild.

After seeing what remained (or didn't remain) of our houses that first day, we drove to St. Rose de Lima Catholic Church and found it still standing (although the steeple was leaning in a very precarious manner). Best of all, Fr. Sebastian was outside talking with some parishioners who had also migrated to the church. Everyone was shell-shocked. Conversations were simple and compassionate, something like, "Are you okay?" The question was asked with great sincerity and great respect in both the asking and listening to the story, i.e. not the bromide type of question when you ask the question but don't wait for the answer. The next question was "How'd you do?" If you said, "Not so good," it meant you lost everything. If you said, "Not so bad," it meant that you could stay in your house even if it was in bad shape. Oftentimes, when something devastating occurs, someone will say, "It could be worse." With Katrina, no one uttered this!

Fr. Sebastian quietly but with conviction said, "God is with us, and we must figure out a way to help our community," and this began the long, rocky, yet amazing journey of recovery and rebuilding. Members of St. Rose mobilized and formed what would later be known as The St. Rose Hurricane Task Force, a rag-tag group of parishioners with Fr. Sebastian at the helm. They transformed our school into "The Hilton" for parishioners, local citizens, and volunteers; the auditorium into a clothing depot; the cafeteria into the best dining in the city; our outdoor pavilion into a Laundromat; and our church into the town hall information center for FEMA, MEMA, National Guard, DMR, SBA, Corps of Engineers, and our hero, Congressman Gene Taylor (he and Margaret lost their home too) to provide critical information to the public. If you needed help or wanted to help, St. Rose Church was the place to go!

The Task Force met regularly for four years to identify and respond to the most current needs of the community as they changed from food and shelter to setting up FEMA trailers to rebuilding homes to rebuilding resilient spirits. At each meeting, Fr. Sebastian would lead us in prayer and then recount amazing miracles (I don't use this word superficially) that had transpired since our last meeting, e.g., the arrival of new groups of volunteers and generous donations from churches, schools, and individuals. Next, we would map out how to respond to the most urgent needs. We came to know and trust in the providence of God, the goodness of humanity, and the support of and for one another. I was honored and humbled to be part of the Task Force—they empowered me, challenged me, and kept hope alive.

Immediately, churches, schools, organizations, and individuals from all across the United States generously responded to our desperate situation and began sending volunteers, prayers, and money to help us. Some churches chose to help St. Rose because of sharing a common church name, e.g., St. Rose de Lima Catholic churches in Hazelhurst, Georgia, in Milton, Florida, in Hastings, Michigan, and in North Wales, Pennsylvania. Some chose to partner with us because of a relationship with a member of our parish, such as Leslie Conwell, Jerald and Lin's daughter and member of Holy Trinity Catholic Church in Washington, DC. Immediately, Holy Trinity adopted St. Rose and across the last five years has sent hundreds of volunteers to help us dig out, clean up, ready yards for FEMA trailers, re-roof houses, float Sheetrock, construct new houses, arrange D.C. respite trips, refresh our spirits, and so much more. They, along with other volunteer groups and individuals, taught us by their actions what it means to be a holy and apostolic church.

Immediately, AmeriCorps, Hands-on-America, Eight Days of Hope, and long-term volunteers such as Brian, Loretta, Beau, Mo Gatto, and the Bucks-Mont Pennsylvania group, Di Fillhart and Bonnie Ringdahl from Pneuma, and Rabbi Myrna Matsa from the New York Board of Rabbis-United Jewish Communities pitched their tents (and campers) among us to help rebuild our communities. In the last two years, Di, Rabbi Myrna, and Dr. Ruvie Rogel from the Community Stress Prevention Center in Israel empowered us to rebuild our spirits and move towards resiliency as individuals and as a community. They have been passionate, unrelenting, and courageous in their efforts to physically and emotionally rebuild the Mississippi Gulf Coast.

Now a few words about Fr. Sebastian (Father, you can't delete this!). While Katrina blew away our community, Father Sebastian was more powerful and breathed life back into us through proclaiming the Good News in the midst of utter devastation, instructing us in ways to love God and our neighbors, and most of all, practicing what he preached! He is gifted with a steadfast faith in God and the people of God, extraordinary leadership skills and business acumen, determination, a playful sense of humor, and the ability to challenge people to be compassionate with themselves and others, and used each of these gifts on a daily basis in guiding us/me in the physical and spiritual recovery, rebuilding, resiliency process post-Katrina. He was, as the St. Rose community proclaims each Sunday at the liturgy, "in the right place, at the right time!"

Some of the *greatest hardships and difficulties* following Katrina were/are:
• Three of my current/former students died.
• Close friends moved away from the Coast.
• Seeing folks visiting their slabs still hoping to find some part of their past lives.
• Needing and accepting help from volunteers who shoveled out the inside of my house and carted flooded appliances and furniture to the street. I was overwhelmed by the reality that I needed help. It was a very humbling experience even though their help was given with great respect and dignity.
• Knowing that it will take twenty years or more for our communities to be rebuilt.

Some of the *greatest frustrations* following Katrina were/are:
• The lack of organized assistance in providing food, water, shelter and fuel for citizens in the initial days following Katrina. This was distressing for me because I am the daughter of a federal worker, born and raised in Washington, D.C., and a believer that we have a fine government. But it was incomprehensible to me that there was such minimal assistance in those early days. Finally, the National Guard and Army arrived by the thousands.

For days there was the incessant sound of helicopters dropping water, ice, and MREs (Meals Ready to Eat) to us. They set up staging areas for distribution of the same items and provided a sense of order in chaos.

I know a lot of folks dump on Wal-Mart, but I'm here to say I was and am grateful to them. Although our local Wal-Mart sustained extensive damages, they had systems in place to immediately set up a tent store to provide essential supplies. Five years later, Wal-Mart remains the only grocery store in the Bay St. Louis-Waveland area!

• Finding housing and having to move four times in four months after the storm.

• The seemingly endless phone conversations explaining Katrina losses to FEMA representatives (thirteen at last count) and SBA loan officers (thirty-five at last count).

• Paying off the mortgage on my destroyed property so that I would be eligible for a thirty-year SBA loan. I am sure I will be the oldest working nurse in US history!

• Dealing with governmental bureaucracy was an abomination, time consuming, a waste of taxpayer dollars, and seriously delayed the recovery and rebuilding of both New Orleans and the Mississippi Gulf Coast. There was a pecking order to having your house, slab, debris, and/or fallen trees removed; homeowners had to obtain a ROE (Right of Entry) certificate awarded by FEMA, who in turn subcontracted with the Corps of Engineers, who then subcontracted with a company from Florida, who in turn subcontracted with Hemphill, who then subcontracted with private individuals to do the work! You knew you were in the system, when the ROE-MSO # was emblazoned in orange spray paint on the entryway of your property but still had to wait months to a year for the work to be performed. On the day Jerald's slab, pilings, and debris were removed, oversight representatives from each of the above-stated entities (no fewer than ten people) watched as three workers performed their tasks. A similar entourage of representatives with heavy equipment came to Devil's Elbow to remove a single dangling limb from one tree, yet they would not remove the two hundred plus trees that were fallen and obstructing the roadway. They were so entrenched with abiding by rules that they could not see or respond to the obvious.

• The most denigrating experiences were working with insurance companies who readily distributed National Flood Insurance Program (NFIP) monies (federal dollars) but engaged in abusive "wind versus water" battles with clients when it came to homeowners' coverage. Their goal was to wear us down and keep the money. Many homeowners are still engaged in litigation or the mediation processes with their insurance companies (I chose the latter route… which is better termed "the humiliation process"). One insurance representative from the corporate office kept insisting I could live on the second floor of my house even though I kept telling her that the Corps of Engineers had demolished the house four days prior! Their behavior was abusive and reprehensible.

• The latest frustration is that Jacobs Entertainment of Cleveland, Ohio, which has some fifty-four truck stop video poker concessions in Louisiana and elsewhere has attempted to rezone an area in my Diamondhead community where more than two hundred fifty homes were slabbed by Katrina so that they can build a casino. According to a vice president of the casino group: "This is a piece of property that's right off the freeway. So access is good. That's important for any business" (WLOX, December 12, 2008). Consequently, this group is attempting to buy out waterfront properties of residents who are still negotiating with their insurance companies and/or who are reluctant and fearful to rebuild if a casino is to be their neighbor.

At a Hancock County Planning Commission Hearing, the casino group claimed that the area was blighted and promised they would bring prosperity to our area. Yet, what they call blight, we call home, and many folks want the chance to go back home. These types of business strategies are destructive, reprehensible, and demoralizing as we attempt to rebuild our communities and lives. There should be laws enacted to prevent these predatory behaviors, or better still, businesses must develop a social conscience!

Some of the *greatest joys* following Katrina were/are:

• Shortly after the storm, seeing my brother Bob and niece Megan arrive from DC in a pickup truck laden with cleaning supplies, shovels, chain saws, and work gloves, which became the inspiration for the St. Rose Tool Loaning Center. They also brought me toothpaste, underwear, and work clothes carefully packed by my niece Erin and sister-in-law Eileen. Bob and Megan helped me dig through the debris and find family treasures (such as my mom's Hummel of The Madonna with Child—unfortunately, Jesus lost his head in the storm and so did I!).

• In December 2005, helping alongside hundreds of other citizens and volunteers to build the first KaBoom Playground on the Coast. The idea was the brainchild of my good friend and neighbor, Jo Gilmore, who was a child during Hurricane Camille and recalled having no place to play. She was determined that life would be different for "Katrina Kids." She met with KaBoom Playground company, and now there are more than 150 playgrounds for children and adults across the Mississippi Gulf Coast and in New Orleans.

• In May 2006, all of our nursing students, the Katrina Class, passed their nursing board examinations. Kudos to these exceptional students and my determined faculty colleagues.

• Getting dirt for Christmas 2007 (the first step in rebuilding) and moving into my new home at Devil's Elbow in November 2008, thanks in large part to my extraordinarily talented niece-architect, Courtney, who designed my new home in Devil's Elbow as well as Jerald and Lin's home in Diamondhead.

• Volunteers who have become lifelong friends, such as Margie, John, Sarah, Brian, Loretta, Adele, Di, Bonnie, Mo, Rabbi Myrna, and Ruvie.

• Fr. Sebastian and my St. Rose community.

The lessons of Katrina...

We all have debris in our lives! While Katrina exposed so much of our external debris, it also challenged us to deal with the internal debris of life. The debris prevents us from being our best selves, being better friends, better neighbors, better citizens. My debris hinders me from forgiving more, trusting more, supporting others more, volunteering more, and trusting God a little more! What helps is to give God a "right of entry" (ROE) into my heart and allow Him to transform me.

I am learning many lessons from the experience of Hurricane Katrina taught by my neighbors, students, the indomitable spirit of the volunteers, and from my St. Rose community. The lessons are how frail and resilient the human spirit is; the capacity that we have to give unreservedly; how to receive help humbly; how to empathize, cry, and laugh heartily with others; that goodness and generosity are the finest characteristics of being human; and God is always with us.

Mary Louise Coyne, born and raised in Washington, DC, is a professor of Nursing at the University of Southern Mississippi. She worked diligently with St. Rose Outreach and Recovery and has been an active member of St. Rose parish. She resides in Diamondhead, MS.

Forever Grateful....

Rhonda Labat

Myron and I have been married for thirty-four years, and Bay St. Louis has become my home. We have been blessed with three wonderful kids and three awesome grandsons. We also have the support of a large and loving extended family and a hard-working church family. I have worked as a medical technician at DuPont DeLisle for thirty years. My husband has worked as an educator and administrator for the past thirty-five years. We are active church members and community servants. We do make efforts to give back to the community that has given us so much.

We love this area because of the easy way of life and the inherent sense of community. Sure, just as in any place or home, there are some problems; but Hurricane Katrina arrived and gave the word "problem" a new meaning. The day before Katrina, our family evacuated to Meridian, Mississippi, to seek shelter at my mother's and sister's houses. Because Katrina's winds devastated the city of Meridian almost as much as the Gulf Coast (except for the flooding), it was four days after Katrina before the roads leading to our home were opened. Downed trees and power lines in central Mississippi, some 170 miles north of the Coast, made travel next to impossible for several days.

Once we could travel home to survey the damage, we were presented with other challenges: fuel lines, fuel shortages, limited supplies for clean up, and rumors of disaster-related crime among other challenges. Upon arrival in Bay St. Louis on September 9, 2005, we were astounded and appalled at the level of destruction. Our home had suffered water damage from the tidal surge as well as from the rain pouring through the damaged roof. Since there was no electrical power in our part of town for two weeks, we could not stay overnight during the cleanup period. In order to clean up our home we, along with a few family members, would make the 240-mile round trip from Meridian to Bay St. Louis and back every day for at least a week. The National Guard closed roads into the Coast area at dusk, and the cities were under martial law. Since the entire Gulf Coast was in the same predicament, we assumed (correctly) that assistance would not come quickly. Following those early post-Katrina days, Myron and I briefly lived with our son and daughter, Myron, Jr. and Cherie, who gladly opened their hearts and their home to us in Kiln, Mississippi. We were, of course, grateful to them but we needed to move closer to home and to what was happening in our area so we could begin the repairs that we needed to make to our home.

Katrina forced us to learn to start over, how to fight, how to cry, and most assuredly, how to pray. The storm uprooted us, making us the "have-nots" who were seeking the bare essentials of food, water and shelter. We wondered where we would get our next hot meal. Thank you Red Cross, Salvation Army, St. Rose Outreach and Recovery, Eight Days of Hope, church groups from Ohio and other places, DuPont-DeLisle, and many others. While we stood in the lines waiting for hot meals, it was apparent that community status no longer mattered. We were definitely all in the same boat, after all. Black, white, Republican, Democrat, Protestant, Catholic—we all bonded together in the aftermath of the storm to face our common enemies: overwhelming devastation and the insurance companies who refused to pay.

When Fr. Sebastian, the pastor of my church, St. Rose de Lima, called and announced that we needed to start a task force for community relief, I was a bit apprehensive. However, I knew from experience that if Fr. Sebastian envisioned it, the plan was destined for success. We started slowly, but our efforts gained momentum as help came from all over the country. An early challenge for us was to find places for all the community members and volunteers to eat and sleep. I volunteered to work serving evening meals for the volunteers as this was a stress release for me and an escape from the close quarters of the trailer we called our post-Katrina home!

Soon we developed a schedule for a group of parishioners to cook meals and get to meet the groups that came to help. My daughter, Marion, also joined the Task Force Team. She volunteered countless hours scheduling volunteers, filing seemingly countless requests for work by the surrounding community as they came in day by day. Marion has always served in the church. She came to work early and stayed late in order to be sure things would run smoothly the following work day. Her hard work and organizational skills earned Marion a position with the group as office manager for SOAR (St. Rose Outreach and Recovery). She worked daily with her three-year-old son, Chris, by her side. During this period Marion gave as much of her time and her energy to the recovery effort and the community as anyone, and much more than most.

Katrina took a lot from us, but it brought wonderful people into our lives that we will never forget. The many volunteers brought with them kind hearts and spirits, as well as skills that helped us repair our homes and our lives. Apparently, someone noticed and appreciated my efforts during the recovery enough to nominate and honor me as one of Hancock County's Ten Outstanding Citizens. While I was truly honored, I was also humbled by the recognition. I felt that my efforts were no more than a small response to the outpouring of generosity our community had received from various parts of the country and the world.

Our "Family to Family" experience with our friends from Holy Trinity Church in Washington, DC was amazing. These families opened their homes for two consecutive years to families from St. Rose for vacations, and they treated us like royalty. They paid for our trips by arranging transportation for two years. My grandson Dedrick and I experienced every tour that was offered in the DC area. I was able to walk in the house where Fredrick Douglas had lived; I stood in the Kennedy Center; I heard Senator Ted Kennedy debate on the Senate floor. These were, indeed, memorable experiences.

Of course there were lots of Katrina-related experiences that I would like to forget. We lost friends, acquaintances, neighbors, and coworkers to both death and relocation to other parts. Throughout the recovery, however, we did make new friends and did find ways to survive and recover. Recovery was tough. During this period my mother would call regularly to remind me to slow down in my efforts to get back to normal as soon as possible, but slowing down was just not an option for me. There was just too much to be done.

The result of our efforts and all the assistance we received is that we are now better as a community than we were pre-Katrina. Much of our community's recovery is due to the dedication and work of the Task Force assembled by Father Sebastian. I am proud of the leadership role taken by St. Rose parish post-Katrina. I am also proud to have had a small part in that effort.

Rhonda Labat is a member of St. Rose parish for 35 years and a career employee of the DuPont chemical company. She has served as Youth Minister at St. Rose for the past four years. She is the proud mother of three and grandmother of three boys. She and her husband of thirty-five years, Myron, Sr. have been living in Bay St. Louis since 1975.

Lasting Impressions
Beau Saccoccia

The South Mississippi of my youth smelled of honeysuckle and jasmine, gardenias and brackish water. In our front yard, rich, green, broad, waxy Magnolia leaves glistened brightly in the sunshine, balanced by its grand, delicate, soft, white flowers. Short-needle pine trees that spawned after Hurricane Camille grew tall during my childhood, filtering the bright Mississippi sunshine down to the crabgrass below. From my bedroom window, I could look through the trunks of those pines, below their canopy, out past the yucca plants to the smooth horizon created by the brown, blue water of the Mississippi Sound. The warm water of the Mississippi Sound gave Hurricane Katrina its last breath of energy before the storm wreaked havoc on the communities along the Coast.

Katrina's powerful wind snapped those short-needle pines in our front yard, laying bare the sandy soil below. Floodwaters lifted our home off its foundation and folded it like an accordion. My sister found my uncle's three-foot-tall plaster sculpture of himself wedged between the kitchen and dining room floors. The water pulled my baseball cards from their home inside boxes and spread them throughout the grass like confetti. The water also carried our dining room table to the back door, where it sat next to my mom's upturned sewing machine and a shelf of cookbooks. That is where I found my mom's copy of *The Joy of Cooking*, one of the few keepsakes that I salvaged from my childhood home.

A year prior to Katrina, my parents had bought a house in Montana, and they were trying to sell our Mississippi home when the storm made landfall. So we gathered what we could, tore the house down, and moved.

Not long after I returned to Mississippi, I found myself in a back pew at my home church, St. Rose de Lima. St. Rose was hosting one hundred volunteers (of which I was one) to rebuild the roofs of twenty parishioners. Tears welled in my eyes when the reader spoke from the lectern, as he/she does at the beginning of every Sunday Mass, "If you're returning to St. Rose after a separation of months, or even years, welcome home." I was home. As always, church members welcomed each other with hugs and held hands during the singing of the Lord's Prayer. Father Sebastian preached lovingly and powerfully, while the gospel choir's soulful songs created space for individual and collective expression of grief and struggle and joy.

A week after that Mass, I stood on top of Dexter Bell's house in the early evening, and I sang along to the radio with a group of volunteers. The gnats had awoken from their midday slumber to chew on our bare legs, and Dexter brought up a pot with a burning T-shirt to keep them away. The sweat dried on my forehead; my shoulder ached from the continual up and down, up and down, up and down the ladder with bundles of shingles; and my hands felt raw from moving shingles heated by the Mississippi sun. From the crown of his roof, I saw trees denuded of their leaves and FEMA-blue tarps on the roofs of the neighbors, and yet I was exuberant. We had just nailed the last of the cap shingles, and Dexter could finish renovating the rest of his home. I sang loudly alongside people I considered dear friends, although I had only known them for a few days.

At first, the work satisfied me for its simplicity. A long day of hanging drywall covered the bones of a flooded home with new skin. So many of us escaped the mundane bureaucracy of office work for the pleasure of a day's labor and the feeling of belonging to something larger. And we were making a difference. We were helping families get back on their feet.

During those months, a few dedicated women ran the parish response to the storm. The school buildings and the church had largely been spared, so it became a natural hub for the relief effort. Racille, Manu, Tini, Marilyn, and Evelyn showed up daily in baby blue shirts that read, "Rebuilding for the Lord" to greet the throngs of forlorn, shocked residents trying to recover. That group of women waited each day until the last person in line had signed up for help.

I once came into the office to ask a question, and I happened to be barefoot. Racille saw me and cackled, "I smell cheese, Beau. Cover up those toes." The women carried themselves with poise and humor, in spite of their own personal loss and the enormity of the disaster.

They'd sit with residents while they cried, or they'd usher residents back to the classrooms filled with canned goods, off-sized windows donated by Lowe's, pots and pans from Saudi Arabia, and paper plates with the stamp of pharmaceutical companies. Donations large and small, useful and worthless, poured into St. Rose; and we'd have to wade through to find what was worthwhile.

There were a number of others from different parts of the country, working together to figure out how to move the relief effort along. Among those volunteers who came and gave their time, I count some of my most dear friends. Brian and Loretta Treffeisen moved to Bay St. Louis (the first time) around the same time I did. We set up camping sites behind the St. Rose Elementary School, in a little corner of the property away from the hustle and bustle. I lived in a tent on palettes with air conditioning and a small front porch with a folding chair. Brian and Loretta set up their pop-up camper next door. Late at night, after volunteers had moved along, we'd play cards, eat ice cream, and trade stories of the day. Each morning, we woke up next to each other, took our outdoor showers, greeted the day's volunteers in the Elementary School cafeteria, worked alongside each other, ate meals together, and spent evenings together. We grew close quickly.

We were contributing something to people who were hurting; we found value and strength in helping people get back on their feet. One elderly man told me he was ready to quit before we came along. At the time, I didn't know where to put that, and I still don't; but it spoke to the urgency of the need. Although we did not seek to put ourselves in the lives and the fabric of a hurting community, once we were there, we felt useful.

The sense of caring stemmed from Father Sebastian's leadership. No matter the time of day or how busy he was, Father always had a moment to listen, to support and to love. Father Sebastian woke every day before six, led morning Mass, and then went to the office where he fielded requests from people asking for help, offering help, looking for guidance, all the while maintaining his duties as a parish priest. He worked until 6:00 or 7:00 p.m., after which oftentimes he had a parish meeting, a city meeting, or a county meeting to attend. Most nights he finished working around 10:00 or 11:00 p.m., with just enough time to fall asleep and start again the following day. On weekends, when we rested, Father was preparing for and leading Masses. Throughout that entire time, he acted with love and care, which made it easy for me to stay at St. Rose for a while.

As the initial adrenaline faded, I realized I was in a unique position to make a longer, lasting impact. One year after the storm, the women who had led St. Rose's effort had returned to their own lives; but more than 5,000 families in Hancock County were still living in FEMA trailers. I knew the area and its people, and like so many others, I wanted to give back.

Thousands of volunteers wanted to help rebuild; funding remained in the St. Rose Relief Fund, and millions of dollars in federal and private grants had been earmarked for rebuilding homes in South Mississippi. Our challenge was to design a program to bring together those resources. I worked with Father Sebastian to devise a plan to keep the St. Rose recovery effort going.

One mile away from St. Rose, the William J. Kelley Retreat Center sat gutted and empty. The site was perfect for our effort. Once restored, it could house two hundred volunteers in small rooms with private bathrooms, and it could house national non-profits like Catholic Charities and the Salvation Army, and it could serve as a hub for residents looking for assistance. With Father Sebastian's blessing, I put together a proposal to renovate the Retreat Center, which The Society of the Divine Word accepted, and our volunteers spent the last months of 2006 renovating the facility.

Our greater task was to direct volunteers in constructing houses, and each day presented a new challenge. Sometimes we had highly skilled volunteers who worked efficiently; other times our volunteers needed more direction. Directed gently and efficiently, I've watched in awe as a group of strangers worked alongside each other to raise a house in less than a week. I've also been amazed by goodhearted volunteers that created a fantastic mess when they used their bare hands to mud drywall. Fortunately, we had willing teachers in Brian and Minnesota Tim, and later in Nicole Pulkkinen to guide the volunteers.

While we were operating at full capacity, we offered families a great opportunity. By rebuilding housing stock, we were not only giving families a safe place to live, but we were restoring their equity and their savings. We rebuilt the homes of families without asking too many questions. Most often, we provided the labor and donors provided the material. When we said yes, families were ecstatic. When we said no, people demanded to know why. To an outsider, our choices seemed arbitrary. Although we gave priority to the elderly, the sick, people with disabilities, people who were financially disadvantaged, our system was inexact.

Stephanie Philips rented a home prior to the storm, so she had not lost much; but she also did not have many options for assistance. One afternoon, Stephanie stormed into the St. Rose office demanding to know why St. Rose wasn't going to build her a home. Stephanie knew we'd helped another person in a similar situation, so why couldn't we help her, she insisted. She'd worked hard all her life, and it wasn't her fault that she belonged to the Methodist Church down the road and not St. Rose. I tried to reason with her, but in the end, I had to admit that I did not know. So I sent her to Father Sebastian. A few months later, we were working with Stephanie to pick out the interior colors for her new home. And good for her.

During the next two years, we rebuilt over three hundred homes for families and hosted thousands of volunteers. As our lease on the retreat center came to an end, the leaves had returned to the magnolias and the oak trees, the piles of debris had been cleared away, but there were still many people in need. I stopped feeling excited and new groups of volunteers came through; I stopped caring about the details of the work; and I was tired. It was clear that it was my time to go, so I moved on.

Looking back, I am thankful for my time in Mississippi, mostly for the people it brought into my life. I came away with lasting friendships, a sense of purpose, and the feeling of being loved that Father Sebastian imparted into us all. The success of our effort stemmed from his leadership, and it grew with the outpouring of support from volunteers across the nation.

Although we lacked experience, we compensated with determination and heart. We shared a common goal to help a community in need, and we came away with deeper understanding of the collective ability to heal.

Beau Saccoccia is a native of Pass Christian, MS where he spent his childhood. After high school, he was enrolled at Dartmouth University, MA where he completed his degree in Mathematics. After his extended work with Katrina recovery organizations and other non-profits, he moved to pursue a Master's degree in Architecture at the University of Texas at Austin.

Forever I Will Sing
of the Goodness of the Lord
Sherry Hill

My name is Sherry Hill, and my most favorite thing to do is to sing. I have been doing this since before I was a teenager, so I have been singing for a very long time with different bands and church choirs. My mother's name is Carrie, and she is now a widow since I lost my dad, Stacy a couple of years ago. I have a brother, Norris, and two sisters, Dora and Annie. We all have our own families, and we may not see each other during the week. But one thing that we try to do is have a family Sunday dinner each week at different homes. Sometimes we're not all there, but those who are manage to have a nice time. We try to stay close.

I was living in an apartment in Bay St. Louis when the storm hit our fair city. Thank God that I left there because I may not be writing this story now. Most of my family had left town for safer areas. I stayed with my fellow church members. My parents' home held up well during the storm, despite roof damage. However, my apartment was a different story. It was totally consumed by water. Needless to say everything was a total loss. All the things that I had were all gone, except my little car, my purse, and the clothes on my body. The job that I had before the storm was suddenly gone. I now had no idea what I was going to do. My life had turned upside down.

I had no idea at that time that I had to go through this to get to a better place in life—that better place that I had always hoped and prayed for. At the time prayer was my only source of strength, along with the kindness and compassion of friends who too had experienced tremendous losses in their lives. At first, there was no idea how things would work out. So in order to begin to make it back, I started praying. I prayed harder than I had ever prayed before, except during the storm. I tried to stay very close to God and to the church, and I began to experience peace within myself. You see, I have been saved by the grace of God. Just knowing that gave me the motivation to pick myself up, dust myself off, and try to get back on track.

St. Rose Church has always been a place of comfort and strength for me. I loved singing with the gospel choir. Having made a turnaround for better with the support of my family, friends, and this wonderful community, I had converted to Catholicism in 2004. After Katrina, St. Rose became not only a place of spiritual support, but also a place for me to live. The school buildings at St. Rose were cleaned up by then and when I asked Fr. Sebastian if I could stay in the classroom, he warmly welcomed me. Soon there were other families who moved into different classrooms in the school. Having Al Acker, the gospel choir director for St. Rose and Goodwill Baptist church, in the same building was a great support. Even in those dark days we sang and gave praises to God for His goodness and mercy.

I lived in that classroom for about four months. Sometimes Fr. Sebastian would come by checking on us to see if we were all right. I began to look for a new job as my previous place of employment at the Dunbar Village nursing home had gone completely under water. My prayers were answered and I was hired at the nursing home in Diamondhead, where I still work, and that felt really great. After I started working I applied for a trailer. When it finally arrived, I went from my classroom flat to my new abode. Although I felt happy to receive the trailer, I actually felt sad to leave the classroom and all the activities that were happening there in the school. While staying there, I was able to witness the kindness and support of people from all over the country. I have never seen so much generosity in the fact that these wonderful human beings put their lives on hold to help me in my hour of distress.

I always wanted to own a home, but I always felt it was out of my reach. Since I was renting prior to the storm, the insurance money for contents was meager. I did not qualify for any grant money. I did not qualify for a Habitat home as I was making more money than their specific criteria for a single person dwelling. It seemed that doors were constantly closing on me. I knew at that time St. Rose was repairing and building new homes. I approached Fr. Sebastian and the director Beau Saccoccia with my request. I was thrilled when they informed that if I was able to secure a piece of property, they would try their best to build a home for me. Rev. Jeffrey Reed sold me a piece of property for a discounted price and that was the first step. God began to open new doors for me as I began to see work done on my newly acquired property. I will forever be grateful for the many volunteers who worked selflessly to build my new home. They built my home from the ground up. This was a wonderful blessing. Then I didn't know where the furnishings would come from. God stepped in again and provided everything that I needed. God is a good God.

My whole recovery process has been one blessing after the other. I find myself constantly saying, "Thank you Lord." When I look back over my life, and where He has brought me from, and how He has kept me, it's a true miracle. He can take you from one point to the next in an instant. That's His miraculous intervention. Sometimes when I'm driving my car, I think about all that He has done for me, and I get so excited that I just start clapping and praising. I have to catch myself and say, "Girl, you are behind the wheel of your car, so get it together." So right now in terms of my recovery I am better. I would like to be more spiritually grown, though. There are things that I would like to share with others that might help them with some problems that they may encounter. Things that I have gone through may be a light unto someone else's path. God wants us to share what we have learned with others. I will continue to always pray, for God has always been and is still very good to me.

Sherry Jean Hill was born in Millen, GA and moved to Bay St. Louis in 1964. She has been an integral part of St. Rose Gospel Choir and Church. Currently she works in Diamondhead, MS. She uses her gift of music to bring joy to many.

And I Remember Kindness

Missy Treutel Schmidt

Both my husband and I are from large families and we love it. He is one of eight children, and I am one of six. Most of our extended family live in Waveland, Bay St. Louis, Pass Christian and Long Beach, Mississippi. It had never dawned on us how important it would prove to be that we lived just ninety miles to the east in Daphne, Alabama.

Ted and I have five children, and in August 2005 they were 18, 16, 14, 12, and 10. He was a pharmacist working at Monroe County Hospital and doing consulting work, and I was beginning my sixth year teaching eighth grade at Christ the King Catholic School. Every day was an adventure in our home. In the mornings I would bring Claire and Emily with me to CKCS as the older children, Chase, Matthew, and Mary Margaret, would head over Mobile Bay to McGill-Toolen Catholic High School. We all tried to work as a team, and we felt blessed in so many ways.

Barely two weeks into the new school year, all eyes were on the coverage of Hurricane Katrina. As the hurricane's path started looking more ominous for the Mississippi Gulf Coast, my sister Cathy, pregnant for the first time, and her husband Steve, along with my sister-in-law Jennifer, with children in tow, headed east to our home for safety. However, more of our extended family decided to ride the storm out in their homes, many of them only blocks from the beach.

As the reality of the massive hurricane became clearer, our family and friends gathered and prayed for mercy and miracles. We were to receive both within weeks and months. Katrina roared through on August 29th, and by evening, no information was available about our extended families or the Mississippi Gulf

Coast. Power and cellular lines were down, and news coverage focused mainly on New Orleans. For a second night we gathered again for a rosary and prayed. By August 30th, word spread that bridges and roadways were washed out, the death toll was rising, and passage was impossible into Mississippi. We prayed a third time for guidance, and God answered our prayer. During the fifth sorrowful mystery, I received a garbled phone message from my brother Paul, who later would tell us he had one flickering bar of cell coverage from the base of the Bay Bridge and hoped his message would get through. Paul stated that Bay St. Louis was no more, but they were all alive and staying near one location in Waveland. That information gave us courage, and it was then that we decided that we as a caravan of seven cars and an RV would take our chances to go help our families.

Christian friends are a wonderful thing. They all seemed to be on the same wavelength. Without power of our own after the storm passed, Ginger next door invited us to watch her generator-powered portable TV set for any news of Mississippi. Once word got out about the caravan at dawn, neighbors and friends volunteered to help. Our pediatrician Gerry and his wife came to our home to give us all tetanus shots for the journey. Marty drove down through the night from Atlanta; Tuerk joined us from Fairhope; and JD brought up the rear with his RV that could carry fifteen people. Not knowing how far we would get and knowing the waters hadn't receded yet, we prayed and turned in for a short night's sleep.

Our first miracle took place as we left at 4:00 a.m. on August 31st. The highway patrol reported that only authorized vehicles would be allowed through the roadways and single-lane bridges. Passing through the Alabama- Mississippi state line, no one stopped us at all. We drove straight on to Hwy. 603, which was still covered with water. As we slowed through the water, we saw a capsized thirty foot boat in the middle of the highway and a car balanced on its nose in a ditch. With the dawn we approached Highway 90 and the first signs of life. Haggard looking people were walking along the major highway pushing grocery carts full of belongings, and others were wringing out their clothes and hanging them on a hotel balcony railing. A few shotguns were propped up against the railings as well. Our hearts sank as we took in this sweet town looking like a war-torn area.

My brother-in-law Steve found his mother in the Waveland Resort Inn. She was in a state of shock and was so grateful we were there. Wet and shivering, she gladly got into the RV along with others of her family members. As we drove further into Bay St. Louis, our caravan had to stop on the highway blocked by power lines and debris in the road. We set out on foot to my sister's home and came upon some of my family, soaked and dirty for two full days, with pets and belongings strewed throughout the front yard. As we gathered them and others from around town, that included St. Stanislaus College, and others, we carried them back to Daphne. One restaurant owner, grateful to be rescued, offered wet money from her cash register for bringing her to safety. Another trip was made the next day for bringing more friends and family. By the following evening, the road blocks and highway patrol were stopping unauthorized vehicles.

Suddenly my home had a new look. As most of the rescued had not changed out of their storm soaked clothes in days, a rotation of showers with bars of soap, toothpaste, toothbrushes, and clean underwear and clothing, all sizes, were awaiting them all as we arrived in Daphne. A very narrow aisle went from the front door through to the back sunroom with money, legal documents and important belongings being air dried by box fans and hair dryers. The first night in Daphne we all gathered at JD's for a buffet dinner and prayed in thanksgiving for all of our blessings, especially the gift of life. After dinner and prayer, we received an invitation to go to St. Paul's Episcopal Thrift Shop, which was opening its doors to us after hours to give clothes, shoes, belts, and more. What a humbling sight to see bankers, stockbrokers, accountants, pharmacists, and businessmen and women and their children picking through racks of donated clothing because they now had only the clothes on their backs. Of their homes, nine were completely washed away and eight were severely damaged.

By the fourth day after the storm, when water and supplies were finally being brought into Bay St. Louis, we had already transported out fifty-four extended family members and eighteen pets to our home in Daphne. Our loving friends and neighbors opened their doors and extra bedrooms to all of our family members. It was such a surreal sight to see all of them walking from homes around the neighborhood in silent march each morning. Each day they would gather in our house, watching CNN coverage of looting in New Orleans and making endless cell phone calls, and in the evenings they would walk down the streets to go to the houses where their beds were for the night. Christ the King School families, parishioners, and Cursillo members as well as neighbors and friends brought a steady stream of breakfasts, lunches, and dinners for everyone to eat. This was our miracle of the loaves and the fishes. Each morning donations of clothing, cell phones, gift cards, even a car on loan for months, and more would appear on our front lawn from school families, businesses, and church groups. The highlight came when a veterinarian offered to discount his boarding fees to take the dogs and cats. Up until that time we had been throwing out handfuls of food onto the deck and hoping that the animals would survive. It was a remarkable sight to see all these animals, strangers to each other, getting along well as if they had sensed an urgent need for unity.

By the end of the week, our pediatrician was busy giving physicals and writing out blue immunization cards to get the twenty-seven high school and elementary relatives and friends into school at Christ the King and McGill. The principals of the two Catholic schools waived the tuition for the year, and donations of books and uniforms flooded in. On Labor Day, the caring owners of a popular Fairhope deli (who had children at CKCS) opened their restaurant after hours for our extended family, friends, church pastor and principal, and served us a wonderful meal. At this point we all took a breath and again counted our blessings.

On September 8th, I remember sitting outside my class-room giving thanks to God and marveling at the way He works. As I prayed, a man walked up from the parking lot and said he was from CNN and was told there were stories to be found over here in Daphne. I took him to my house, and he interviewed each of the seven transplanted families individually.

As the first acute phase was ending, the second phase began. Our parish church, Christ the King in Daphne, would leave messages at school informing me of people willing to open their homes to our displaced families for longer durations. One by one, the Treutels, Taylors, Kergosiens, and Schmidts found lodging in longer-term homes all around town. Some were staying in homes on the Bay; others were in mother-in-law suites in Fairhope. Rental homes and apartments were hard to find, but by God's grace, we found several. God was working overtime for us all.

As the school year progressed, my eighth grade class, which had nine Katrina refugees at one point, asked to travel to the

Mississippi Coast and offer a work day to the parishioners of St. Rose Catholic Church as their class gift to the school. They also voted to donate carpeting to St. Rose Church, donate an LCD projector to Our Lady Academy in Bay St. Louis, and bring a monetary gift to St. Clare Church in Waveland. Our principal, Sr. Maureen, agreed to their requests and allowed the students to raise the funds. On January 27, 2006, nearly five months after the storm, a bus load of seventy-five students, teachers, and volunteers spent the day raking and cleaning yards around St. Rose and distributing over $6,800 in monetary gifts. The parishioners of St. Rose, opening their homes and tattered yards to us, were so gracious and gave much love and affection, especially to the youngest volunteers. One homeowner gathered the students working for him in prayer as the work day ended. Before boarding the bus, Fr. Sebastian welcomed the volunteers into St. Rose and gave a word of thanks and praise, and pointed out the beautiful carpet that our donation had made possible. The testimony from all of the students was profound. They were so moved to be able to help in some small way, and many were to do it again and again.

In time, the Mississippi schools and businesses began opening again, and a few of the families went back to clean up and rebuild. Other families would stay until December and still others would remain until the school year ended in May 2006. Finally, some of our extended family would make Daphne their home. With all that happened during those weeks and months following Katrina, I will never forget the kindness of friends and neighbors, and the tangible hand of God.

Missy Treutel Schmidt was born and raised in Bay St. Louis, MS. She and her husband Ted along with their five children cherish living in Daphne, AL for the last 20 years. Missy is grateful to God for her local community who joined hands with her in reaching out to the people of her native town, Bay St. Louis, MS.

"This Is Church"

Jeffrey Reed

I can vividly remember that day in August of 1969 when Hurricane Camille slammed into the Mississippi Gulf Coast. It was an adventurous day for a boy my age. People were boarding their windows and doors, fueling their automobiles, and doing last-minute grocery shopping. They were preparing for the worst but hoping for the best. At approximately 6:00 p.m. that evening, the lights began to flicker, both the wind and rain intensified and it was downhill for the next four to six hours. I remember lying in bed that night listening to trees falling, branches breaking, and rain drops being blown against my window pane by Camille's violent winds. The sound is forever etched in my memory. What a night!

The next morning, nothing could have prepared me for what I was about to see. As my daddy and I walked around the city (because driving was impossible), I was amazed at the amount of destruction and devastation a hurricane could cause. I saw trees, some two hundred years old, plucked up by their roots and removed from their original location by Camille's twenty-five foot tidal surge. Power lines were down, cars were crushed, and buildings flattened. From that moment, Camille became the measuring stick and the mother of hurricanes, that is until August 29, 2005, some thirty-six years later.

On that day a hurricane named Katrina slammed the Mississippi Gulf Coast, bringing with it a storm surge of more than thirty feet. This storm caused the nation to halt, as it covered approximately 250 miles of coastline and three states, and reached hundreds of miles inland. Hundreds of lives were lost. Churches, houses, and schools were damaged, destroyed, or declared uninhabitable. This storm is now the mother of hurricanes and the measuring stick by which other hurricanes will be measured. Much can be said about Katrina's wrath and its aftermath, but I want to tell you about the miraculous role of the church in the midst of this horrific disaster.

"Church" is first mentioned in the Bible in Matthew 16:18 where Jesus says, "Upon this rock I will build my church; and the gates of hell shall not prevail against it." "Church" is from the Greek word *Ekklesia* (Ek-klay-see-uh) from which we get our English word "ecclesiastical." The literal meaning is "a called-out people." This church, that Jesus said He would build, would be something new and different. He would unite believing Jews and Gentiles, forming a new body wherein natural distinctions would be unimportant. He would call out a people from all backgrounds, nations, and tongues—a people with no denominations, prejudice, or racial barriers—and use them to show forth the love of God to a hurting world.

This is the miracle that Katrina revealed. The church is not a building with stained glass windows and padded pews. It's not a structure with high ceilings and fancy brickwork. The church is a called-out people who have the heart of God and minister the love of God to a hurting world.

The church didn't receive much media coverage after Katrina, but she responded to the dilemma as the Samaritan responded to the man left half dead. Luke 10:33-34 says, "But a certain Samaritan, as he journeyed, came where he was; and when he saw him, he had compassion on him, and went to him, and bound up his wounds, pouring in oil and wine, and set him on his own beast, and bought him to an inn and took care of him." You see, this is church! They came to where we were, they saw us, observed our dilemma, and they had compassion on us. The church (the called-out ones from across this nation and the world) poured in healing oil and wine, they bandaged our wounds, and they took care of us. This is church!

The church moved across the disaster area with skill, precision, and most of all love. The church left the comfort of their air-conditioned buildings, came out from behind the four walls of their million-dollar facilities, rolled up their sleeves, swatted the gnats, and endured the heat. They set up feeding kitchens, hosting thousands upon thousands for breakfast, lunch, and dinner. Some even worked into the midnight hours, feeding and caring for the police officers and first responders. I saw the church not just *send* relief but *bring* relief. They did what Jesus said: they laid down their lives for others (a people they didn't even know) by sacrificing vacation time and family time. They bought Sheetrock, insulation, water heaters, paint, and so much more. They left the comfort and luxury of their homes and cities to make our homes and city what it used to be and better. This is church! They spent their Thanksgivings and Christmases with us to bring some normalcy to our lives. They bore the cold winter nights sleeping in tents, showering and bathing whenever and wherever possible. They rolled up their sleeves, gutted houses, cleaned yards, and poured out their hearts; they had compassion on us. By joining forces with the National Guard and city officials, the church and government walked hand and hand with common goals—rebuilding lives and revitalizing our cities.

So we along the Gulf Coast region can all say with a unified voice that—had it not been for the church (that called-out people)—we would not have recovered as quickly as we have. Thank God for the church, the body of Christ that is fitly joined together and every joint supplies (Ephesians 4:16).

Bishop Jeffrey Joseph Reed is the Founder and President of the Power House of Deliverance Ministries in Bay St. Louis and Picayune, MS. He is the author of two popular books (Bent Nails and Chipped Bricks and From the Cave to the Throne). He currently serves as Bay St. Louis Councilman for Ward 3. He and his devoted wife Tina have four daughters: Stephanie, Kendra, Tamara and Christa.

Eight Days of Hope

Steve Tybor

A miracle in the dictionary is defined as a "wonder" or "supernatural." My definition is slightly different. A miracle to me is when God moves in such a way that you stand back in awe or amazement of who our God is and how He can open doors that you never even thought existed! You stand back and ask yourself, "Did that really happen?" Of course it did—not because of us but because of HIM! This is the story of Eight Days of Hope.

In the first week of September of 2005 as I was watching the destruction and aftermath of Hurricane Katrina on TV, my phone rang. Living in Tupelo, Mississippi, my dad called from Buffalo, New York, asking me if I would be interested in going to the Gulf Coast with a friend or two to help in the rebuilding process. I found that a little amusing because he knew that I had never operated a tool or handled a hammer in my life, yet he felt we could make a difference.

I hung up the phone with him and started to ask myself, "What can one person do? What could five or six of us really accomplish? Could God use five men to impact a family or maybe even two families on the Gulf Coast?"

Have you ever witnessed a miracle? Have you ever seen God move in such a mighty way that you step back and say WOW? We soon were to realize that it wasn't about a father and son going to the Gulf Coast, but it was to be about a movement of God that would eventually touch thousands of people's lives and impact families forever. Our God is a God of miracles and the story of Eight Days of Hope was starting to take place.

I shared the passion with some of my friends here in Tupelo, and there seemed to be an interest in people wanting to come

201

with us. I started to realize that maybe five or six would not be going, but maybe we could have as many as twenty to twenty-five people going and making a difference in the name of Jesus! God started to bring together the leadership team as He used people who knew each other (from near and far) to shape a leadership team that would lead His ministry! God brought a home-schooling mom, a banker, a teacher, a local businessman with a heart for missions, and others to spearhead what now seemed to be a passionate group ready to do its part in the rebuilding process.

My dad and I realized that we needed a name for this group. Yes, it would be a onetime trip but we thought it was wise to give it an identity. The number eight means "new beginnings." When we considered the real reason we were going to the Coast, it wasn't necessarily about rebuilding the damaged homes, but it was about sharing the hope of our God! We wanted to tell them that He would never leave them nor forsake them and that He will be with them at all times even during and after a hurricane like Katrina. He is a God of Hope! "Eight Days of Hope" had been born! Praise God!

Isn't it a coincidence that American Family Radio is based in Tupelo, Mississippi? One of the largest Christian radio networks in the world was right down the street! Believe me, our God is not a God of coincidences. He knows exactly what He is doing! He was about to display His first miracle to us!

More than two hundred radio stations around the country are committed to broadcasting God's Word and Christian music every day. We decided to approach AFR about running a local spot to try to attract some more volunteers. I met with Tim Wildmon and shared the passion that was on the heart of this small leadership team. He too wanted to make a difference, and that meeting changed our plan for this ministry like I never would imagine. AFR saw the passion and seemed impressed with the game plan that God had given us. In that next sixty minutes, AFR committed to helping Eight Days of Hope put together a website, airing spots across the nation, and promoting this mission trip to the coast of Mississippi. God, can this be? We never expected this type of support! This is starting to get interesting! The meeting was a huge success; and to this day when we ask a volunteer how they heard about Eight Days of Hope, most mention AFR. Yet, God wasn't done on this day showing favor to us.

Don Wildmon, the person who started American Family Radio, asked to see me. When we met for a couple of moments he asked about our plan and asked about the accountability we would have over our finances. I thought to myself, sure we will have accountability, but what finances was he talking about? At this point we had about $3,000 to take with us to buy materials. After answering a series of questions, he told me how excited he was about what God was doing and that AFR wanted to be a strong supporter of Eight Days of Hope. He handed me an envelope and asked me to be a good steward. He said that a thousand dollars was a lot of money, but he knew we would spend it wisely. I thanked him and went on my way.

I sat in the parking lot in my car with an envelope in my hand praising God for the favor He had just shown us. I opened the envelope so I could stop by the bank and deposit the check only to catch my breath. The check was for $100,000, not $1,000! Are you serious, Lord? I must have misheard Mr. Wildmon. I was sure he said a thousand, not a hundred thousand! $100,000! "To much is given, much is required." God's Word clearly ran through my head as I started to sob. God, why would you grant us this miracle of favor and finances?

Armed with radio exposure across the country, dollars in the bank, and volunteers starting to pour in from across the country, we needed to see where God would take us and who we would partner with as we were getting ready to take the next step of faith. Our prayer was simple—God please direct our path; show us clearly where to go and who to work with. After praying, God started to open door after door.

Frank Scott, a local businessman and I drove to the Coast just ten days after the storm. Television did it no justice. The damage was surreal. Was this a hurricane or a nuclear bomb? We drove to different cities on the Coast and in Gulfport we were escorted to an area that was not open to most. The smell of death was in the air. My heart sank. The tears flowed all morning long, but during this time God started to show us who Eight Days of Hope would partner with.

We had multiple meetings that we had set up prior to arriving. Every meeting was a blessing as God started to open up doors for the lodging we would need for our volunteers. After all, our volunteers had grown from twenty or thirty to three hundred! They would need a place to sleep and we also had to wonder how we would we feed them. I couldn't help but remember the story I heard many times growing up—the story of Jesus with the fish and the bread feeding thousands! Our God had more miracles ahead for us!

God clearly showed us that He wanted us to spend most of our time in Bay St. Louis and Waveland, Mississippi. Our paths crossed with St. Rose de Lima, First Baptist, and other churches in the area. God struck friendships almost immediately and trust was built between people who have never met yet had one thing in common. We all loved God, and we all wanted to serve those who needed help in the name of Jesus!

We decided to use the churches in the area as our contacts with the families that needed help. They would introduce us to the people in their congregations who did not have insurance or who had suffered unbelievable loss. We then asked these churches to pick some homes in the area of people who did not go to church. Our goal was simple—we wanted to show these people the love of Christ! We wanted this group to know that God had not forgotten them.

Eight Days of Hope went to the Coast of Mississippi in December 2005. What was meant to be a small group of people turned into an army of volunteers from forty-two states totaling more than 650 people. They came in all shapes and sizes, different denominations, and different skill sets; yet God opened the doors for this group to help rebuild eighty-four homes! That in itself is a miracle! How does one coordinate rebuilding eighty-four homes with people they just met? How do you do all of this and be protected from injury? Jesus! It's that simple!

We prayed with people, cried with people, and yes, we laughed with people. We invited the homeowners back for dinner and to join us in a devotional time filled with worship! It was a time of reflection and a time of hope! Not a hope that man brings, but a hope that only God can bring.

God had supplied us with places to sleep, food to eat, and the building materials that would allow us to accomplish all that He wanted us to accomplish.

Driving home after that week made us realize that God would not have opened these doors if He only meant for us to do this one time. God clearly showed us that we were to continue to trust Him and lean on Him as we were to go back. We heard Him loud and clear, and unanimously decided to form an organization that has since been on seven trips to four areas of the country.

Four times we visited this Katrina-devastated area of the country. Through Eight Days of Hope, God led more than

3,500 volunteers to our new home away from home. The amount of work that God allowed us to do is staggering. On these four trips we were able to finish more than 800 projects and accomplish over six million dollars of work with the cost of materials and donated labor.

This is not the only miracle God displayed. Eight Days of Hope was always meant to be a conduit for believers to share the gospel, to share Christ's love. Lives have been changed, hope has been restored, faith has been renewed, not because of us per se, but because of Jesus!

The enemy tries to tell us that we don't matter, that we could never make a difference in the world on behalf of our Lord. That is a lie—one big fat lie! We can make a difference! God is waiting for us to follow what He has shared in Scripture when in 1 Peter 4:10 He says that we are to "use the gifts that God has given you to minister to one another." What is your gift? How are you using it to glorify Him?

Eight Days of Hope is a story of moms, grandparents, teenagers, and yes, contractors, remodelers, builders, and plumbers using the gifts God has blessed them with to bring hope and the love of Jesus!

It was meant to be a small onetime trip of men to the Gulf Coast to fix a home or two. God had bigger plans. Much bigger plans! Trust Him for the miracle in your life He has planned for you!

To God be the glory!

Steve Tybor resides in Tupelo, MS with his wife, Charmaine and their three children: Stephen, Zachary and Hannah. Though originally from Buffalo, NY, they have made Mississippi their home for the past 11 years. He is employed as the sales manager for a company in Boonville, MS. He is very excited to see where God takes "Eight Days of Hope" next!

The Miracle of Two Chairs

Margie Legowski

When Katrina hit the Gulf Coast, I was a single, white, Catholic, and fifty-plus woman on a week-long prayer retreat, trying to come to grips with a floundering love relationship, my mother's dementia, and my shaky faith and tendency to the negative. I was totally and painfully directionless and self-absorbed. I didn't have access to television, newspapers, and radio, so it wasn't until I was halfway through my drive home that I learned that Katrina had devastated the Coast.

As I drove and listened to countless news reports from New Orleans (of course!), something shifted and I felt a not-so-gentle pull to do something. Little did I know that that pull would lead to a life-changing relationship with my parish, with a place called St. Rose de Lima, with myself, my job, and, most importantly, with God.

How did I get involved? What did I do?

Two weeks after Katrina I showed up at Holy Trinity to help load the truck taking cleaning supplies, gift cards, and requested clothing to Bay St. Louis, and met Frank Monahan, a Katrina Task Force member and a voice of reality and parish wisdom. In the middle of a discussion about our joint Peace Corps roots, I found myself asking if I could go down to St. Rose and offering to help him and the Holy Trinity Task Force think through a plan to send down volunteers. What strikes me now is that I didn't even think the words—they just seemed to come out of my heart.

The Task Force, which was made up of many of Holy Trinity's leading parishioners, intimidated me at first. But I learned over the next four years to trust, love and argue with this unique group of passionate people—all of whom had been touched by the people of St. Rose de Lima. They were: Frank, Cathy Quinn, John Bradshaw, Pat and Charlie Betts, John Hisle, Maureen Leventhal, Trish Swift, Sarah O'Neill, Adele Baker, Leslie and John Conwell, Kevin O'Brien, SJ, and our pastor Jim Shea, SJ. Many other wonderful people such as Marty Walsh, Travis Brown, Chris Knauer, and Mary Phillips Quinn also seemed to show up exactly when we needed them. All were welcome there.

Although we each brought unique gifts to the Task Force, the person who never called attention to herself, Leslie Conwell, brought us the greatest gift of all: the gift of a connection to St. Rose de Lima parish in Bay St. Louis. Things would have been very different had it not been for the Conwells and their family and friends in Mississippi—particularly Jerald and Lin Jackson (Leslie's parents), Mary Coyne, Marilyn Smith, Bruce Northridge, Teeny Williams, Rhonda Labat, Father Sebastian, SVD, and the many others who so graciously opened their hearts and shared their lives with us.

This connection to St. Rose became an incredible source of faith, joy, challenge, and growth for me and for the hundreds of volunteers from Holy Trinity who either traveled to the Gulf to muck out, wire, or roof homes, or help the young people in the Boys' and Girls' Clubs. They coordinated regular Katrina fundraisers; addressed and stamped envelopes for personalized Christmas notes; solicited donations for new appliances, bedding, gift cards or items for St. Rose's church fair; arranged programs and visits to Washington, D.C., for boys, girls, or families; opened their homes to St. Rose vacationers; reminded parishioners to pray for those impacted by the storm; and did a thousand other things that I can't now remember.

Parishioners of all ages (including the school students) participated in Holy Trinity's Katrina response in whatever way they could. No action and no prayer was too small—and all actions, successful or not, brought us closer to one another, to the people of St. Rose de Lima, and, most importantly, to God.

So, what were the miracles in my experience of Katrina?

Whenever I think about my visits to Mississippi, the words, "I myself have seen it" immediately come to mind. Yes, it's true: I myself have seen and felt God's presence in the people I've met and experiences I've had in Bay St. Louis. I myself have seen it.

I'd like to share with you a few of the times when I felt God's presence and saw glimpses of the kingdom. Were they miracles? I believe so. I myself have seen them.

Moments of Connection

In November 2005, on the weekend before I was scheduled to leave for Mississippi, I asked my mother and the other residents in her group home, if they would be willing to help me bake cookies to take down to St. Rose for the Thanksgiving concert reception. I explained where St. Rose was and what had happened as a result of Katrina. They listened intently as I did so and then agreed to help.

This was a miracle. Each of the eight women in the home was in some stage of Alzheimer's, and many also had a physical illness. They were in their late eighties and nineties, and although they'd lived rich and productive lives, they were now being cared for twenty-four hours a day and had little opportunity to give back. The first miracle was that I asked them to help me (where did that come from?). The second miracle was that they all said yes.

I will never forget the image of my mother, Ruth, Lillian, and the other residents bent over the dining room table working painstakingly to shape the dough into perfect cookies for people they didn't know and would never meet. They were alert, engaged, committed, and in the moment, not in the past. God's grace was in that room. I myself saw it and I felt it. This was another miracle.

. The Transformative Power of Faith

I arrived in Bay St. Louis a few days before Thanksgiving so that I could help out and also gather information to share with the first group of Holy Trinity volunteers. Or so I thought. I think the real reason, though, was because I just needed to be there. Somehow, God felt closer when I was at St. Rose. God was in the faces of the people on line at Camp Katrina, in the clasped hands held high during the St. Rose liturgy, and in the work of Bev, Marilyn, Barb, Ron, Rhonda, and others who showed up every day to sort through mountains and mountains of donated clothes and goods so that they could feed the hungry, clothe the naked, and repair the plumbing even when they themselves were struggling. God was in the children who laughed in spite of the chaos around them and in the single butterfly that landed on the bush beside the old rectory. Yes, I wanted to be at St. Rose.

As for the concert? St. Rose was packed on the night of the concert and as the service began, the air was heavy with fatigue and sadness. But as the group sang and choir members stepped forward to sing their private prayers, the atmosphere suddenly changed. The singers stood taller, their voices sounded stronger, and the congregation began to sway to the sounds of hymns that suddenly had new meaning. By the end of the evening, the church and all who were in it were transformed and at peace. God's presence was palpable that night. God had pulled us through yet again. I myself saw it. I myself felt it.

Two Chairs on a Beach

Two chairs on a beach do not a miracle make, you are probably thinking. But you are wrong, my friend, very wrong.

On Thanksgiving afternoon after a busy morning and afternoon, Marilyn and I drove along the beach looking for a place to have a picnic of leftovers. As we approached Waveland, we spotted two Adirondack-style chairs sitting a few feet from the water on either side of a little white table. All three pieces of furniture were undamaged and standing upright, unlike just about everything else we'd passed on the road that day.

We claimed them, set out our meal, and for a few blessed hours, the destruction and needs of the world faded away. For the first time in years I knew that I was exactly in the right place at the right time. I was precisely where I was meant to be, and with gratitude, I recognized the gift of the present moment. It was a miracle to this work-crazed Washingtonian, and I will never forget that feeling of peace and rightness.

The Unexpected Gift

For some reason, this last experience is difficult to write about. Indeed, whenever I've tried to tell anyone about it, I've gotten choked up and haven't been able to proceed. So, what happened?

I returned to Bay St. Louis that December and again in January and March. I remember missing my father a lot during that time (he'd died in January 2001 and his birthday was in March so thoughts of him were always close to the surface during those months).

One afternoon, another Holy Trinity volunteer and I drove over to the Depot for something and encountered a man, who was about the same age and build as my father, wandering around in the parking lot looking tired and a little dazed. I remember being in a hurry and heading to the door of the Depot trying to ignore this man. But something or someone pulled me back, and I found myself going over to ask him what he was looking for and if I could help him. He needed to pay an electric bill, and amazingly I actually knew which trailer he needed. We chatted for a while and, as I turned to leave, he reached out his arms, held me for a moment, and uttered, "I love you." I turned away as the tears started to come. When I turned around again, he was gone.

Was there a miracle here? Probably not by most people's standards or definition. But to me? Oh, yes. There was a miracle that day. My Father comforted me and reminded me of His love just when I needed it most.

It's true: these glimpses of God's presence and love and these reminders of the importance of living in the present moment could have happened anywhere and to anyone. But, you know what? They didn't.

Has the experience of Katrina and this St. Rose connection changed me?

Almost five years and twenty trips later, the answer is definitely, "Yes! Yes! Yes!" And the changes were both professional and personal. I thank God for that from my heart.

Professionally?

Yes, I am better at my job—I am able to interject a little St. Rose perspective into discussions about coordinating and counting volunteers during a disaster; and when a disaster hits in any part of the world, I feel pain and a longing to help and try to do something, even if it's just to pray.

I signed up to be a member of my Agency's Disaster Cadre, a team of staff members trained to deploy under FEMA mission assignment to help coordinate volunteers in disaster-torn parts of the country. As a result of that, I spent a month in Baton Rouge during Gustav and Ike helping to coordinate volunteers for a call center for a pilot project. I couldn't have answered those phones and listened to the people on the other end, had I not seen Bay St Louis and Waveland and heard the stories of my friends there. Each person I encountered in St. Charles or Terrebonne parish, Louisiana, was a Marilyn or Teeny or Mary or Lily to me—and not just a number on a form.

And when the earthquake struck Haiti, I found myself again in a call center, only this time in Washington, DC, and on the opposite end of things. This center was for people who wanted to volunteer, or donate clothing or helicopters, or somehow do something. I recognized the need to respond in those who called and was now able to say with conviction, "These are some of the things you can do with your church," and "No, please don't send down clothes right now (thank you, Bev!—she organized the items at St. Rose' distribution center)—there's no place to store them; find out what people need first."

And personally?

I now know in my heart and not just in my head, that while things are nice, they're not that important. From seeing Marilyn and her mama and grandbabies, I learned in my heart that family and faith matter, and I have tried to make time to attend to both. From Mary, who quietly goes around helping her students and many others, I re-learned the meaning of generosity. And from the entire St. Rose community, I learned in my heart that God is the only constant and the source of all love and strength. God will, indeed, pull us through.

When I look back over my time in Mississippi, I realize that I saw glimpses of the "kin-dom" while I was there: people working together, people reaching out to strangers, people being lifted up one more time by their prayers and their faith. I myself saw these things. It was a miracle.

Margie Legowski is a member of the Holy Trinity Parish, Washington DC, where she has served on the Katrina Task Force and other ministries of the church. A former classroom teacher, she has taught in the U.S., Denmark and Sri Lanka. She served in the Peace Corps from 1987-89 and has been with the U.S. government since 1990.

Faith of the Heart

Tish Haas Williams

I will be the first to admit it. My life is out of balance. I spend too much time working, not enough time focused on my financial future, and my kids are home alone too often. I don't exercise, don't eat right, and I live a stress filled life. But, I must be doing something right. Balancing all of life's challenges is a daily struggle. For so long, as a major control freak, I tried to control everything. The fact is, my life was and still is in many instances out of control.

When I was thirty-six, I was on my way to the top, only two steps away from that big title, corner office, and six-figure salary. Yet, I saw life passing me by. I realized that while I was grabbing for all of the gusto, I was about to let one of life's most important roles slip right through my fingers.

I have to experience everything life has to offer, I thought. *How can I go through life and not experience motherhood?* And, my husband agreed. Together, we set out to make it happen. I followed every rule; met every deadline; and, using the power of prayer and scientific intervention, I became pregnant against all odds. Today, my husband George and I are the proud parents of thirteen-year-old twin daughters. Tricia and Georgia are our pride and joy. We cannot imagine life without them. And, because of them, our lives have changed forever.

When the girls were first born, I found myself still focused on my career without integrating my new role as mother. I was flying all over the countryside, working too much, never seeing my husband and new babies. Why was I focused in this direction? The honest truth was that I was dedicating my life to an organization that could have easily replaced me. As I began to come to this realization, the real question became: "Could I re-

215

place my husband? My children? My family? Could they replace me?"

One day, one of my employees set me on a completely different path from where I was heading. I noticed that she was always so organized, so together, so deeply spiritual. How did she do it? Desperate, I asked her to share her secret with me. It was the Franklin Covey System of defining what matters most to achieve your highest priorities. At the age of thirty-nine, for the first time in my life, I sat down and developed a blueprint for my life.

I actually thought through and answered three simple questions: What really matters most to me? What is the source of my passion in life? Where should I focus my energies? All of my answers came back to family. Yet, most of my time was spent away from my family. I was living in Baltimore, Maryland, thousands of miles away from my brothers and sisters, their children, and my parents. My children would grow up without that solid foundation of family that has always been my rock. Let's face it, your family will love you—warts and all—when no one else does. They will support you when you make mistakes and, trust me—we all do. But how could I make my family my priority and get off this roller coaster? Suddenly, everything I had worked my entire life to achieve was no longer important. Immediately, I went to work to set out goals for my life.

"I want to be a better wife, mother, sister, daughter, person!" (This is a daily struggle. My family says I never answer my phone or emails. I'm working on it. But, I am always ready for a family cookout or a night on the town.)

"I want to eat healthy and exercise." (I am still working on this one too. I have joined at least five gyms in the last ten years and have made it to each one at least one time before never going back. And, I always sign up for a one-year membership.

And, I know, I am overweight and have high cholesterol. I'm not perfect. But, I am happy. Is there anything more important?)

"I want to raise my children in my hometown—Bay St. Louis." (This was going to be even tougher than making it to the gym more than once a year. My husband and I both had great jobs in Baltimore in specialized fields. How would we transfer these skills to a small community, still make a decent living, and be professionally fulfilled?)

"I want to get closer to God and build my faith." (I remember dragging two baby seats up two flights of stairs to the baby room at church. When the girls were five, and they could walk on their own two feet into church, I literally had an epiphany. I saw God's plan for me unfold before my very eyes. He had sent me around the world to end up right where I had started. Along the way He had equipped me with every skill I would need to face the greatest challenges of my professional career.)

Oddly enough, the first job I was offered right out of college was director of the Hancock County Chamber of Commerce. I turned them down. I was going places. I wasn't going to stay in this small town forever. I was going national! I remember thinking I had a national calling, not really knowing why I thought this. But I left, worked for several different national organizations, and did not really return to live in the Bay area until 2000. In 2002, I was offered the job as director of the Hancock Chamber of Commerce. Hopefully, the first job I was offered will now be my last.

Let's face it; no one has a perfectly balanced life. My work still dominates my time, and I think my family has just come to accept that this is my calling—this is what fuels my soul—and they integrate in to my work and truly support me. We like to call it the "art of living."

I still stumble with my faith, never feeling equipped to know how to properly pray and ask for my blessings. (I'm Catholic! My parents, Myrt and Mike Haas, gave all of their six children a strong foundation of Catholic traditions. We went to church every Sunday and Catholic school from kindergarten through the twelfth grade. And over the years, I admit, I drifted away from my faith. I was even mad at God and the church for a long time. A lot of good that did me.)

Ancient text says: "The masters in the art of living make little distinction between their work and their play, their labor and their leisure, their mind and their body, their education and their recreation, their love and their religion. They hardly know which is which. They simply pursue their vision of excellence in whatever they do, leaving others to decide whether they are working or playing. To them, they are always doing both."

When I needed help from a higher power, I went to my mother. (Please understand, I am not suggesting that she is the "Higher Power," although some may beg to differ. But, she was and still is my direct connection to the ultimate Higher Power—God). I asked her to intervene on my behalf with her prayer group, half wanting to believe yet never really understanding how the power of prayer could really work. Yet I saw it work for her and her group of Steel Magnolia friends over and over again.

There are three significant events that produced powerful results through the power of prayer that truly turned my life and my faith around.

At thirty-six, I finally realized that I really wanted to become a mother, and I did. In fact, in my case I think God said, "Well you're out of time so I'll just go ahead and give you both children at once." I was thirty-eight when the girls were born. Two years later, we found out my husband had prostate cancer.

Cancer really shakes you up and makes you focus on what is really important. I love my husband and I did not want him to die of cancer; today, eleven years later, he is still cancer free. I guess God said, "How can she make it without you, George? She still has a lot to learn from you and so do those girls!"

Another year and a half later, I started thinking about where the girls would go to school. I began to dream about what I wanted for them in their lives. I began to think about my childhood and how wonderful it was to grow up on the beach in a small town; to know the love of your grandparents and your aunts and uncles; to grow up with your cousins, swimming, sailing, going to the beach; riding your bike around town—exploring life. I wanted the same things for my children—but where was this place?

George and I were still living in Baltimore at the time. That weekend, I was flipping through *Coastal Living* magazine and I turned the page and saw the headlines: Best Place to Live: Bay St. Louis, Mississippi. I said, "What?" I had gone halfway across the United States only to find out that the best place to live is right where I grew up. "Okay, Auntie Em, next time I won't look any further than my own backyard!" That night, no joke, the Wizard of Oz came on TV.

I said, "Okay, call the prayer line off, Myrt. How can we get home to raise these children?" We were literally starting to lose our y'all! The "get me home prayer" garnered the quickest response. One week after sending this prayer up, I had a new job; and a month later, I was moving home to Bay St. Louis. I am not kidding.

In each case, my mother's prayers were answered. How did she do that? She has the power of faith—faith that the Lord will provide all of your needs. And, when you believe, He will. She told me later that she had actually been working on this prayer for quite some time. Opening the door was up to me.

Five years later, in 2005, my hometown was hit by the nation's worst natural disaster—Katrina. Close your eyes for just a minute. Think about your office, your home, your personal belongings, family pictures, the little things that make your house a home. Now, open your eyes and imagine all of those things gone, overnight. That is what happened to the people of the Mississippi Gulf Coast. Overnight, I became the director of the Chamber of No Commerce.

All but two of the eight Chamber offices coast-wide were destroyed. Two hundred people were dead. More were missing. All communications were lost, and the entire seventy-five mile beachfront was devastated. Destruction from wind and rising water extended more than fifty miles inland. The lives of 400,000 survivors were changed forever. Today, almost five years later, we pause to reflect on how far we have come. And we look to the future to continue to rebuild our communities—one business, one home, one day at a time. With 65,000 homes destroyed and 55,000 more housing units initially damaged coast-wide, it is far from over even five years after the storm. While it is a painful and slow process, we have made it to several major milestones.

Only two weeks after the storm, the Chamber reemerged as the first Business Assistance Center on the Mississippi Coast, bringing all of the resources for small businesses together under one roof. We were the window to the world for our businesses and residents—providing access to the Internet, and phone and fax services. Small Business Development Center counselors from across the country came to help our businesses reconstruct their financial papers to apply for SBA disaster loans. Volunteers from the International Economic Development Council came in for years, offering technical advice and assistance. Through our efforts, the Hancock Chamber was recognized nationally as a model for disaster recovery; and in 2006, I was honored to receive the National Phoenix Award by the U.S. Small Business Administration for Outstanding Service by a Public Official. When the President of the United States showed up at the Awards Presentation, I realized it was a big deal. We weren't setting out to win awards, we were just making it up as we went along, and we did what we could to help our businesses get back up and running as quickly as possible.

Last year, the new bridge that connects us to the rest of the Mississippi Coast was rebuilt and is a beautiful symbol of our recovery. It received more than 25,000 of the 50,000 votes cast for the National People's Choice Award sponsored by AAA, the US Chamber of Commerce, the American Association of State Highway and Transportation Officials, and by the National Transportation Association. It features a walking path and the most unique display of local art found anywhere.

Today, we are at a turning point in our rebuilding. The infrastructure has been completely rebuilt, and all of our roads are being replaced. It still looks like something out of the Wild West in some places; yet in other areas it is a new oasis of beautiful landscaping, new roads, sidewalks and homes. A new beginning.

It is our small businesses I worry about the most. They were hit the hardest and given the least opportunities to survive. Even with $5 billion allocated for Katrina recovery, there has been next to nothing for the small business owners—except loans on top of more loans. Out of the 1,800 businesses countywide, all were shut down, and fifty percent were severely damaged or destroyed. Many did not have business interruption and flood insurance.

A natural disaster, and in this case, a catastrophic event, could affect any one of us at any time. Overnight, business owners who worked a lifetime to build their businesses, found themselves starting all over again with nothing except hope, faith, and a drained retirement account. Today, almost five years later we have just been approved and have launched a low interest/forgivable loan program for small businesses that will help rebuild the retail and service sector of our economy. We have never given up. "Failure cannot cope with persistence" is our mantra. Our customer base was severely impacted by the loss of population, the second home market, and weekend visitors. We are the closest coastal town to nearby New Orleans and the areas surrounding that city.

The beach road, our welcome mat to our downtown in Bay St. Louis, is now partially rebuilt and open. It will take another year to complete. We are literally rebuilding two downtowns from the ground up. The downtown in Bay St. Louis was partially destroyed, and the downtown in Waveland was totally washed away. Local governments have been approved to receive Community Development Block Grant funds to build a waterfront development that includes a harbor in Bay St. Louis, and in Waveland a retail accelerator project will be established to restart the new downtown near the water's edge at ground zero.

To make our communities more inviting, trees are being planted throughout the major corridors. Our trees were among the hardest hit from Katrina. Thousands of trees were lost, and those left are being infected by a rare disease that threatens their very existence. A bright spot is the sprinkling of artistic creations carved into the trees we lost, like the angels that once saved the lives of three of our citizens and their dog.

Part of our recovery is centered on our two hundred resident artists. We are one of the top small art communities in the country. In the aftermath of Katrina, in spite of all that is in evidence around us, we are painting, dancing, singing, writing, drawing, printing, sculpting—we are creating. Through our far flung sons and daughters, angels and volunteers, Katrina established a national marketplace for our artists. To date, our artists have exhibited their works, many Katrina-related, at Alexandria, Virginia; Washington, D.C. twice; Rome, Georgia; New Bedford, Massachusetts; New Harmony, Indiana; Doylestown, Pennsylvania; Amherst, Massachusetts; Southern Pines, North Carolina; Jackson, Mississippi; and New York City.

Another unmet need is housing. There was no single agency in our area to coordinate assistance for low/moderate income housing. Through the Chamber, during 2007 and 2008, we nurtured the establishment of the Hancock Housing Resource Center to get people back in their homes to reestablish our population, labor market, and customer base for our businesses. The Hancock Housing Resource Center has now spun off into a separate nonprofit entity with a qualified board, president, funding, and staff support. We have accomplished much, and we have a long way to go before recovery and rebuilding are complete. We did not get here on our own. It was the people from throughout the country who came to help and who still today give us so much hope. The volunteers knew before we did that a community without hope would have many challenges that federal assistance could not address. And the people of Hancock County are eternally grateful.

When you witness firsthand the power of the human spirit, people helping people, you know beyond a shadow of a doubt that there is a God. And He has a plan for each of us, whether we are leading a balanced life or a life that seems out of control.

Tish Haas Williams, a native of Bay St. Louis, returned to her hometown in 2000 with her husband, George, to raise their twin daughters. She became the director of the Hancock Chamber of Commerce in 2002 after gaining 20 years of experience in non-profit management and marketing, skills that would prove invaluable to the community when Katrina devastated Hancock County.

Like a Sunflower

Wendy McDonald

I moved back to Bay St. Louis after Hurricane Katrina, leaving behind my doctoral work at the University of Texas in Austin, my dean's position at a large community college in Northwest Houston, and the comfortable career path and lifestyle I had in Texas.

The first five months after Katrina, I lived with my eighty-year-old parents in their FEMA trailer prominently located in the front yard of my gutted out childhood home. Two of my three children along with my parents lost everything. In fact, every single person I knew lost everything they owned.

I hold bachelors and masters degrees from the University of Southern Mississippi and a PhD from the University of Texas in Austin. I felt I had talents that I could share with the community. I formed a small non-profit that hosted numerous public information meetings, provided advocacy for emergency housing, and offered disaster recovery assistance. As there was no Habitat presence in the community prior to Katrina, I also began working with Habitat for Humanity. I now serve as Executive Director of Habitat for Humanity Bay Waveland Area, Inc. serving Hancock County, Mississippi; and I was recently elected to serve Ward 2 as Councilwoman for the city of Bay St. Louis. Under my leadership the Habitat affiliate has built over one hundred forty homes, and we have raised well over $15 million dollars for the rebuilding effort in Hancock County.

When asked how I dealt with the aftermath, I usually answer that I thrived in the post-Katrina environment because there was so much to do and there were funds to accomplish our goals, but it was hard to be patient.

The great part about the recovery was the nonprofit partners that helped carry the load. The Hancock County Chamber of Commerce opened their doors to provide free office space with phone lines, fax machines, copiers for businesses and non-profits to share. This was a blessing! Watching the Chamber staff, especially the Executive Director, Tish Williams, coordinate and assist with recovery efforts beyond the mission and scope of a Chamber of Commerce was inspiring. Lagniappe Church was helping families we could not help; St. Rose Outreach and Recovery was doing inspiring work for local families. Together the load was lighter. The relationships that developed among the nonprofit leaders were incredibly helpful both spiritually and emotionally. We "got it" in a different way, a boots-on-the-ground way.

The part of the recovery that was so difficult was the waiting and the frustration over the rules that applied to disaster response and rebuilding. Knowing the money was there but not being able to quickly access the funds was mentally exhausting. Rules that were written for regular hurricanes and normal size disasters were trying to be applied to Katrina and made no sense. That was so unbelievably frustrating that many of us found we actually had to take a therapeutic pause, a refresh and renew weekend, to keep from losing our effectiveness.

The volunteers that reached out to our community were amazing, they came with such giving hearts and embraced our community with open arms—we all just marveled at these total strangers that just showed up to help. They brought our stories back to their communities, they brought us their joy of giving, and they loved our little town at its shabbiest, dirtiest, and ugliest moment. They could see that it was worth saving! That was endearing. It also helped us not feel forgotten—we were feeling like the world thought the only city impacted by Katrina was New Orleans.

There are so many Katrina stories, we all have them—some are funny and some are just a series of recollections that aren't particularly funny or sad, they just stick out in our minds.

My days for the first few months after Katrina consisted of waking up about 5:15 a.m. in my parents' FEMA trailer, selecting an outfit from one of my allotted sixteen hangers in my closet, and heading off to try to get a newspaper before they sold out at 5:45 a.m. I would take a different route every morning to check on the progress of the debris cleanup. I loved those few moments every morning because the early morning mist shrouded the debris piles, which turned pink as the sun rose, and it was pretty for a few moments. I think God was giving us a beautiful sunrise every morning to start our day!

The college I worked for allowed me to take a Katrina sabbatical and come home for nine months. One day in March 2006, I was giving them my weekly update, sitting on the steps of a hairdressers shop waiting for my appointment. My boss asked me what I would do in June if I was back at the college, and my community were to have another hurricane warning. I told her I would be right here in Bay St. Louis. I realized right then I needed to resign. It sounded like an instantaneous decision, but I think deep down I knew I wouldn't be able to go back to Houston. They probably knew that too! My work there seemed unimportant and irrelevant compared to the work I was doing here. My heart was here, and I never gave a second thought about my decision to quit.

I love to tell this story of a little miracle that boosted our spirits and brought a few smiles to our faces. Our town was so pretty, dominated by the colors sky blue, lawn green, and nautical white. Now our "eye candy" was stained brown and grey from all the salt water and mud. I remember driving along the beach and only looking to the right—out over the Bay—to give my eyes a much needed rest from looking at debris fields and dead trees. However, one day in early 2006, big, fat sunflowers started blooming all over town, in the middle of debris piles, from under broken piles of collapsed homes, in oily, nasty roadside ditches. They grew everywhere. It was as if they had personality, their heads tilted this way and that as if they were looking back at you, smiling. You had to smile back. It was just the silliest looking flower. Sometimes I would see one and just laugh out loud. I didn't want anyone to give me the rational explanation—the bird feeders were full when the storm hit and the seeds flew all over and were buried in the mud. I believed it was God giving us something to smile about and giving us a symbol for our recovery. We were those sunflowers: survivors, funny, cheerful people, and just a little muddy.

Wendy McDonald is a native of Bay St. Louis. However, she has lived and worked for many years in Texas as a college educator. After Katrina she moved back to Bay St. Louis and volunteered her time with different organizations. Currently she serves as the Executive Director of Habitat for Humanity Bay Waveland Area, Inc. She is an elected City official for Ward 2 in Bay St. Louis.

Gratitude—A Life Transformed

Rabbi Myrna Matsa

It does not look the same. You can read a newspaper or a news magazine, even watch television coverage and it is not the same. From these you only have an inkling of reality but without the textures, sights and smells. November 1, 2006, I was sent to the Mississippi Gulf Coast and Louisiana by the national Jewish community. The job was to be a pastoral presence and to work with religious leadership who were providing spiritual support to their communities post-Katrina and Rita. At the beginning it was mostly to companion rabbis and cantors and immediately expanded to working with interfaith clergy of all denominations in the region. Little did I understand how this work of holiness would change my life. I came to help and was helped in the process.

When I arrived fifteen months after Katrina struck the Gulf Coast, there still was evidence of the destruction. Dead trees lined the highways as their skeletal remains soared upward toward the sky. Remnants of people's histories and private lives could be found in the tangle of tree limbs. But much progress had been made toward clearing the debris and roads to make pathways accessible for transportation and emergency vehicles. BellSouth was in the process of restructuring the telephone grid because the telephone and electrical systems had been completely destroyed. You could not find the *New York Times, Wall St. Journal,* or *The Economist* at the neighborhood book dealers because roads were broken and transportation costs were high. Grocery stores were not fully stocked. And places like Bay St. Louis still did not have a grocery store.

Homes had been wiped off the face of the earth and so had evidence of their ever having existed. Buildings of all kinds and their contents had blown away in the torrent of wind and water; this included schools, universities, hospitals, houses of worship, museums, offices, libraries, historical landmarks, service stations, and homes. People lost their history, which significantly altered their view of the future. Grief abounded. As people assessed their losses there were a variety of responses. Some realized that "stuff" was what they lost, but others grieved the loss of irretrievable memorabilia such as photos, important documents, personal and public history. There were the dead to be grieved. There were friends, neighbors and coworkers who evacuated before the storms and stayed away. Those losses created opportunity to think about life and meaning. Many people came to reconsider their values and their goals.

I have been altered by this experience and am privileged to share a small portion of the reason why. The first time I had been in Mississippi was for the job interview in September 2006. I was drawn to the work; I wanted to be part of the recovery. And yet I was somewhat conflicted because of memories of Civil Rights struggles, the movie *Mississippi Burning* and news reports of years past that now feel as though they were long ago. I knew that I would have to confront my own stereotypes. However, from the first moment I came to the region I found the people of Mississippi to be warm, welcoming, and overflowing in gratitude. Regardless of the hardships encountered, most folks were grateful. Mostly they were grateful to have survived Katrina. In their gratitude they reached out to each other.

I have never seen so much goodness in my life. It is estimated that more than one million hours of volunteer labor has gone into the recovery of Southern Mississippi. It is acknowledged that faith-based organizations have been one of the major contributors to the recovery. People of every faith and of all ages, races and economic backgrounds have contributed to the rebuilding. They have come as individuals, in small and large groups; they have come as representatives of secular and religious organizations. They have come because the need was and continues to be so great, and they wanted to help. They slept on bunk beds in camp-style barracks; they worked long days in terrible heat and humidity. Rather than complain, they sang and rejoiced because they could see that they had made a difference in another person's life. Often, they helped total strangers.

This is one of many similar stories. Eighteen months after Katrina, Rebecca[1] came with twenty-five other Jewish volunteers from United Synagogue for Conservative Judaism (USCJ). They took vacation time to spend a full week to muck out buildings, bleach mold and mildew, rake yards, and surf the rubble for personal treasures. Sometimes the volunteers met the homeowners and worked together, most of the time they did not. Too many survivors were still in shock and enduring emotional and physical challenges due to bureaucracy with insurance, FEMA, and laws and details. The work of these volunteers could save a homeowner $5,000-10,000, which meant that whatever compensation might come to them could be spent on rebuilding the house.

Most of the volunteers had to be trained and had to be cleared by their physicians. This work was hard and could also be dangerous. At the end of each day, the USCJ volunteers gathered to discuss the day's work; they studied religious texts to put into context the values they were living. Rebecca shared a profound lesson. In her words, "It was life changing." She was raking the debris placing it into piles. One spot seemed to reflect the sun's rays. It was like a beacon of light calling her attention. Gently she removed the debris with her gloved hand and was astonished to find a porcelain teacup without a scratch or chip. Nothing else of the household contents remained. Everything else was destroyed. She washed the cup and set it aside. She knew that the owner was meeting the group of five who were working on this house. They'd meet the owner at the end of the day. When homeowners and volunteers meet, it can be intense. Often there is awkwardness because you are doing something for a stranger and you do not know how they will react or how you will react. There could be a clash of values: on one hand, there is personal joy knowing that you are seriously helping another person; but on the other hand, there can be embarrassment because it is almost like an act of charity and you do not want to demean the person or contribute to their embarrassment. Our volunteers were trained to be sensitive to the owner's needs and to not do anything knowingly that might diminish the owner's humanity.

Later that afternoon they greeted each other. Introductions were made. The owner was amazed that the house that needed so much work on Monday was now fully gutted, bleached, and ready for the next stage of work. She expressed gratitude in such a way that the volunteers shared that they did not know how to respond. The owner spoke from the depth of her heart such that the volunteers began to understand their role in a whole new way. They had come from across the country to do the work of *Tikkun Olam* (Hebrew for "Repair the World"). Our religious texts understand our world as broken and we see ourselves as partners with God, and we find holiness in repairing that which is broken. Until that encounter, Tikkun (repair) had been a concept. In this brief encounter, hearts were united. God's presence could be felt by virtue of one person reaching out to help another.

Then, Rebecca brought out the teacup. This was greeted by a gasp and tears, followed by sobs. This woman in her late six-

231

ties thought she had lost everything. This porcelain teacup was part of a set from her deceased grandmother—it was the only tangible evidence of her childhood, her marriage, her life history. The two embraced knowing that they would be connected to one another forever. Rebecca said to me, "This is why I was put on earth! I have purpose!" Within an instant she understood that the greatest joy in life is when we are in service of others. God's presence can be felt in this exquisite coming together. One can search for God only to realize that God is always with us. It is up to us to unclog our hearts, to remove the blindfold from our eyes and plugs from our ears. Rebecca felt profound gratitude for the privilege and opportunity to be part of this woman's reunion with the teacup. Had she not volunteered, would she have discovered this deeper purpose? I have listened to many similar stories from countless volunteers and also neighbors who continue to care for one another. Shopkeepers, nurses, and teachers among others—many tell stories of how they helped each other and have made a difference in each other's lives.

Hate is when we close ourselves off from ourselves and the world. Love opens us to possibility and others. Gratitude is the deepest form of love that equips us to continue reaching out. In gratitude we realize the gift of life and search for personal meaning. One cannot command gratitude. Our prayers and sacred texts plant the seeds of gratitude. The heart transformed by profound gratitude is forever altered.

It is with gratitude in my heart to be blessed to be a vessel through which the Divine has worked. Through my work I have been privileged to bring people together so that they can sustain each other. I have been able to match needs to resources in such a way that I helped religious leaders so that they had someone to turn to. This enabled them to be more present to their flock.

Rashi, a Jewish medieval scholar, said, "Naked a man comes into the world, and naked he leaves it; after all his toil, he carries away nothing—except the deeds he leaves behind."[2]

The beacon of light from the teacup is a metaphor for how I understand St. Rose de Lima. This beautiful little church building survived the storm to become the hub of community spiritual healing. May Fr. Sebastian and SOAR be blessed in all their endeavors for the ripples of goodness they have brought into this world. Though Fr. Sebastian is not Jewish, he has lived the promise of Tikkun Olam—Repair of the World by his philosophy and practice.

1 The name is fictionalized because I do not have permission to give the real name.
2 *Wise Words: Jewish Thoughts and Stories Through the Ages*, Jessica Gribetz, p. 29

Rabbi Myrna Matsa came to Mississippi in 2006 as part of the National Jewish community's effort to bring comfort to the people of the Gulf Coast. She soon began to work with clergy of different religions and denominations. One of her greatest achievements was to obtain funds from The Jewish Federations of North America (formerly known as United Jewish Communities) to implement Resiliency training and programs for the people and leaders of Hancock County in partnership with the Israel Stress Prevention Center.

And the Journey Goes On...
Di Fillhart

As the winds blew and the waves brought destruction to the Gulf Coast of Mississippi, I sat in Scranton, Pennsylvania, at the Door of Hope Ministries Board meeting experiencing the storm of my life. My beloved husband and partner in ministry had chosen another life path, bankruptcy loomed on the horizon, and pain and devastation swirled around as the board made the necessary changes to move forward. In the lobby of the hotel, a television displayed the massive destruction Katrina had left in her wake.

In July 2005, a month before Katrina, my friend and fellow ministry board member Bonnie Ringdahl had a vision from God in which there was great devastation and enormous need following a storm. Although we had no idea where or when this would occur, we truly felt God leading, so another board member opened their garage, and we began collecting cleaning, medical, and food supplies. It was like Noah building the ark; we kept filling the garage with no storm in sight. Yet when Katrina entered the Gulf of Mexico, we all realized this was what God has been preparing us to respond to.

On August 30, we filled a ten foot trailer with all the supplies we had collected and headed to a place that we had access to and had not received a lot of assistance. During the next couple of weeks we distributed supplies and helped, yet in our souls we knew we had not arrived yet at our final destination. Two weeks after the storm we met the president of City Team in a gas station. We had been praying for an organization that could use our help for a year, and they had been praying for someone to lead their disaster relief work on the ground in Bay St. Louis for a year. God began the tapestry.

As I worked in the distribution center set up by the City Team Ministries, serving 1500 families a week, my soul was longing for the fellowship of a church. That week, seven people invited me to attend St. Rose de Lima Catholic Church. I had never attended a Catholic Church before, and the opportunity was irresistible. Sunday morning arrived; my tired body could not quell the anticipation of my spirit as I walked into the church.

My first memory of that day was the resurrected Christ mural on the wall behind the altar. I gasped at the beauty, the perfect resemblance of what I had envisioned in my mind so many times. As I took a seat in the pew, the quiet reverence for the holy captured me in an encounter that I am grateful for every day. Music erupted as the Gospel Choir worshiped, and here in this humble place, people who had nothing left but their God rejoiced in His faithfulness. I bowed in adoration with them realizing how much we had in common. We had lost loved ones, homes, dreams, and hopes and yet as the disciples said, "Where have I to go but with You." As I look back on that day, I realize how God had divinely orchestrated my life that I would come to be His wounded healer in this place and be healed myself. God is good!

Christmas of 2005 was the pivotal transformation point of my journey of faith. Christmas Eve morning as I sat reading my Bible, I was impressed by the Spirit that I was to invite Christ into the "manger" of my life. Christ's birth in the manger is such a glorious and miraculous event; however, when He left the manger it remained a place with straw, dung, and hay, and was not changed. Only those who found the Christ in that place were changed. I realized that my prayers had been centered on God changing the "manger" of my life—the places of pain, betrayal, humiliation and despair. As evening approached I surrendered my will for God to change the situation and found Christ in the midst of the storm, just like the believers I had met at St. Rose. Christmas morning shone brightly, and as I walked to the church my heart was full of anticipation. When I got to the church, no one was there. Highly unusual for 8:30 a.m. on Sunday! I gently opened the door and slid inside. The presence of God enveloped me; I fell on my knees and sensed His great love and compassion. Minutes became eternity as I lie prostrate before the throne. After what I sensed was hours, I rose and walked out of the church, only to find that five quick minutes had elapsed since I had walked in, and my life had been forever changed. I knew I was the beloved of the Lord and heard Him singing over me (Zeph. 3:17).

Following that day, I continued my pilgrimage each Sunday to St. Rose, drawing and encountering Christ deeper and deeper. During this time I faced the pain of divorce. As a God-fearing Christian woman, I wrestled with deep anguish over God's hatred of divorce and how that would affect my relationship with Him. Father Sebastian, (the pastor of St. Rose Church), reached out to me after a service and asked me if I was okay, which I was not! I made an appointment with him that week for wise counsel about the situation. As we traveled through the Scriptures, his insight into the Word and compassion for my pain brought forth healing and courage for me to take the next steps on this journey of life. From that moment I knew for the first time in my life I had found a pastor, one who truly was the shepherd of this flock and seriously took his position before the Lord with humility and sought the Lord with all his heart.

On Advent Sunday 2007, I sat writing in my journal that I would deny God nothing. Of course at the time I had no idea what nothing involved and no idea that it really meant giving everything to God! Father Ken Hamilton celebrated the Mass that morning; as I walked up in the communion line to receive a blessing, he laid his hand on my head, then reached and held up the host and said, "This is the body of Christ, do you want it?" A wrecking ball took down the walls of my soul and I surrendered again. What was God asking me? The gentle whisper of His Spirit said, "This is home." I called Father Sebastian on Wednesday morning, after three days of fasting and prayer and said "Help! God is wrecking my life and I think I am supposed to become Catholic!" Easter of 2008 I celebrated my conversion to Catholicism; I surrendered my ordination papers and continue to deny Him nothing.

During that time Beau Saccoccia had decided his season here in the Bay was coming to a close and SOAR was looking for another Executive Director. At the Task Force meetings at St. Rose, Elaine Maxion, the case manager for SOAR kept saying, "Turn up your hearing aids, God is calling you!" Sure enough, by April I heard His voice and accepted the call to help lead SOAR on the journey to helping create stronger healthier community in Hancock County! There are so many amazing things that happened during this time, but one event will stand for all time as the hallmark of community in the Bay!

Hurricane Ike had slipped by the Gulf Coast of Mississippi in the fall of 2008 with minimal impact. However southern Louisiana and Texas, which had been hard hit by Hurricane Rita in 2005, were again devastated. The day following the storm, people began calling and arriving at the SOAR office and saying, "When are you going? What can we do? We must do something for them! How horrible it is for them to be building back and be destroyed again! We must help!"

During the next five days, the office was filled to the max as people from St. Rose and the community brought in food, cleaning supplies, and medical supplies. Habitat Bay/Waveland and Lagniappe joined us, and during the next month we sent three truckloads of supplies to Cameron, Louisiana. SOAR also sent a team of AmeriCorps workers and our staff to help set up a distribution center and begin the process of mucking houses and cleaning up. Our commitment to Cameron lasted long beyond the initial response as one of our own staff members, Jim Miller, remained on site for over a year helping the recovery effort. "To whom much is given, much is required." God taught me during the Katrina experience that the miracle of finding Him during the "much," whether I view it as positive or negative, is what is required. A deeper knowledge of His love and the willingness to be His "Earth Suit" began to be the picture of the tapestry.

As the recovery plodded on, infrastructure was reestablished, and homes were rebuilt; but there remained a significant void in the recovery. The sound of laughter was still infrequent and distant; new homes did not have pictures on walls; people felt guilty because even though they had recovered, there remained the sadness of loss, the dismal hope for the future, and the silence of the Katrina event. I attended meeting after meeting searching for a solution.

The answer to my searching and prayers came in the most amazing way! I met Rabbi Myrna Matsa, who was serving the Gulf Coast Community. She represented the New York Board of Rabbis and had a passion to work interfaith. She listened to my concerns and quickly connected me to a Resiliency Training Program in Biloxi being conducted by Ruvie Rogel from the Community Stress Prevention Center in Israel. In a few short months, the vision of training local leaders from government, education, business, and the arts quickly gained momentum. Rabbi Myrna connected SOAR to the United Jewish Communities who embraced our vision with a $100,000 grant.

By the fall of 2008, SOAR hosted the first community resiliency training event. We were blessed by the enthusiasm and
support of the local school system, business leaders, and the arts.
During the next year we hosted 33 training sessions, had 328
participants and 23 individuals became certified trainers, including guidance counselors, clergy, and local residents.
Resiliency is defined as "The Art of Bouncing Back." This became our theme and passion. On our final training session in
December of 2009, we gathered for a community resiliency day.
The weather outside was frightful with rain and storms—how
fitting that we would recognize the resilient leaders of Bay St.
Louis that night. They are the shining hope of the future of the
Bay, bouncing in the rain, during the storms, and every day to
make the Bay a better place. And so the journey goes on, always
seeking deeper the love of God, being His love in the world
around me, and helping those around me bounce back higher
and with lots of shine!

*Di Fillhart is the Co-Executive director of PNEUMA-Winds of Hope Inc.
currently serving in Bay St. Louis, MS. Prior to Katrina she served in NYC as
a Pastor and Missionary to the homeless of Bushwick and Bed/Stuy in
Brooklyn. She continues to radiate the love of Jesus with everyone she encoun-
ters.*

About the Author

Sebastian Myladiyil, SVD, a native of India and a naturalized citizen, is a Divine Word Missionary priest. He has been working in the Southern Province of the Society of the Divine Word in the United States since 1999. He began his ministry at St. Edwards/St. Jude Church in New Iberia, Louisiana. He served as pastor of St. Rose de Lima Catholic Church, Bay St. Louis, Missisippi, for nine years and recently earned his Master's degree in theology from Notre Dame Seminary. Under his leadership St. Rose became an important place in the relief and recovery efforts after Hurricane Katrina.

He was a member of the Mississippi Governor's Commission for rebuilding Hancock County. Through St. Rose Outreach and Recovery (SOAR), an organization established by Fr. Sebastian, more than 5000 volunteers helped more than 500 families. He was recognized as one of the Outstanding Citizens of Hancock County in 2007 by the Hancock County Chamber of Commerce.

Currently Fr. Myladiyil serves as the pastor at Immaculate Conception Church in Liberty, TX. He published his first book *His Instruments—If God Could Use Them He Can Use Us* in December 2009, which was very well received by the readers. Plans are underway in writing his third book.

To contact the author, e-mail him at sebymy@hotmail.com.